TAXING ENERGY : WHY AND HOW

OECD
OCDE

INTERNATIONAL ENERGY AGENCY

The International Energy Agency (IEA) is an autonomous body which was established in November 1974 within the framework of the Organisation for Economic Co-operation and Development (OECD) to implement an international energy programme.

It carries out a comprehensive programme of energy co-operation among twenty-three* of the OECD's twenty-four Member countries. The basic aims of the IEA are:

i) co-operation among IEA participating countries to reduce excessive dependence on oil through energy conservation, development of alternative energy sources and energy research and development;

ii) an information system on the international oil market as well as consultation with oil companies;

iii) co-operation with oil producing and other oil consuming countries with a view to developing a stable international energy trade as well as the rational management and use of world energy resources in the interest of all countries;

iv) a plan to prepare participating countries against the risk of a major disruption of oil supplies and to share available oil in the event of an emergency.

---

* *IEA participating countries are: Australia, Austria, Belgium, Canada, Denmark, Finland, France, Germany, Greece, Ireland, Italy, Japan, Luxembourg, the Netherlands, New Zealand, Norway, Portugal, Spain, Sweden, Switzerland, Turkey, the United Kingdom, the United States. The Commission of the European Communities takes part in the work of the IEA.*

ORGANISATION FOR ECONOMIC CO-OPERATION AND DEVELOPMENT

Pursuant to Article 1 of the Convention signed in Paris on 14th December 1960, and which came into force on 30th September 1961, the Organisation for Economic Co-operation and Development (OECD) shall promote policies designed:

— to achieve the highest sustainable economic growth and employment and a rising standard of living in Member countries, while maintaining financial stability, and thus to contribute to the development of the world economy;

— to contribute to sound economic expansion in Member as well as non-member countries in the process of economic development; and

— to contribute to the expansion of world trade on a multilateral, non-discriminatory basis in accordance with international obligations.

The original Member countries of the OECD are Austria, Belgium, Canada, Denmark, France, Germany, Greece, Iceland, Ireland, Italy, Luxembourg, the Netherlands, Norway, Portugal, Spain, Sweden, Switzerland, Turkey, the United Kingdom and the United States. The following countries became Members subsequently through accession at the dates indicated hereafter: Japan (28th April 1964), Finland (28th January 1969), Australia (7th June 1971) and New Zealand (29th May 1973). The Commission of the European Communities takes part in the work of the OECD (Article 13 of the OECD Convention).

FOREWORD

Energy taxes have considerable currency as a tool to achieve environmental objectives. Governments accustomed to taxing energy to raise revenue or for security may contemplate taxing energy to discourage its use, and implicitly, to reduce energy-related pollution.

Decisions about incentive taxes should not be made in a vacuum. The wish to use energy taxes as environmental policy tools requires an understanding of the existing array of taxes affecting energy, a profile of energy use, and a profile of energy-related pollution.

The energy-related tax levels and structures in different OECD countries are likely to elicit different responses to policy actions, including actions intended to harmonise taxes. Efforts at tax reform or in coordinating environmental and other actions should take these variations into account. Reform efforts must weigh carefully questions relating to internalisation, tax neutrality, harmonisation and the implications thereof. They need also to consider infrastructural investments, and the economic and technological appropriateness of using energy as a proxy for pollution.

This study neither advocates nor opposes the use of energy taxes as a means to achieve government policies. It explores energy tax regimes of selected OECD countries to discover why and how energy is taxed, how susceptible present regimes are to new uses, how effective energy taxes might be for purposes other than raising revenues, and compares them to other incentive mechanisms.

The IEA has been assisted in the preparation of this publication by officials of some of its member countries. I deeply appreciate their help, without which the work would not have been completed. This work is published on my responsibility as Executive Director of the IEA and does not necessarily reflect the attitudes or positions of the IEA or its Member Countries.

Helga Steeg
Executive Director

ACKNOWLEDGEMENTS

This report was prepared by the IEA's Economic Analysis Division. Critical review of the document was provided by the following tax and energy experts from member countries:

Peter Biggs, Francesca Kibiria, Beryl Cuthbertson and John Daley of Australia; Claus Andersen, Ole Bilde, Jens Holger Helo Hansen, and Anita Jakobsen of Denmark; Knut Kübler, Frank Neumann, Elmar Clouth and Rainer Goergen of Germany; Masamitsu Kawasumi, Mitsuru Ota, Jun Arima and Mikio Kajikawa of Japan; David Hatcher, Linda Radey and Bob Conrad of the United States; Diego Piacentino of Italy. The IEA Economic Analysis Division worked closely with the OECD's tax experts.

The IEA wishes to acknowledge gratefully the assistance of these reviewers, who were particularly generous with their time and efforts.

TAXING ENERGY : WHY AND HOW

TABLE OF CONTENTS

Foreword   5
Acknowledgements   7
Table of contents   11
Summary   13

Introduction   15

PART I
CASE STUDIES   17

A.   Australia   21
        Energy tax profile   21
        Energy profile   36
        Energy-related pollution profile   41

B.   Denmark   45
        Energy tax profile   45
        Energy profile   56
        Energy-related pollution profile   61

C.   Germany   65
        Energy tax profile   65
        Energy profile   72
        Energy-related pollution profile   80

D.   Japan   83
        Energy tax profile   83
        Energy profile   92
        Energy-related pollution profile   96

E. United States   99
    Energy tax profile   99
    Energy profile   111
    Energy-related pollution profile   116

PART II

**ENERGY TAXES AS POLICY MEASURES
IN THE CASE STUDY COUNTRIES**   119

A. Energy taxes as fiscal measures   123
    - Raising revenues   123
    - Redistributing income   127
    - Capturing rents   128

B. Energy taxes as non-fiscal policy measures   130
    - Taxing to reduce consumption   130
    - Taxing to change consumption/energy
      security   137
    - Taxing to reduce energy consumption-related
      pollution   141

PART III

DEFINITIONS AND CHOICES FOR ENERGY TAX REFORM   155

A. Internalisation - taxes and other instruments   157
B. Neutrality   162
C. Appropriate proxies   164
D. Harmonisation   168
    Competition and Harmonisation   171
    CO_2 taxes - A special case   173

SUMMARY

This publication attempts to do two things: first, to open a dialogue among member countries about the role of energy taxes as non-fiscal policy instruments; and second, to provide, by using case studies, a factual background for what would otherwise be a theoretical discussion.

From a fiscal point of view, governments tax energy to raise general or earmarked revenues. From an energy policy perspective, governments may tax energy to affect fuel mix, promote energy production or conservation, encourage security of energy supply or reduce energy-related pollution. Energy taxes and subsidies can also be used to protect and promote the interests of domestic industries.

The study examines energy taxes in five OECD countries in light of the above, to see why and how energy is being taxed, and how effective governments might be in using energy taxes to achieve their various fiscal, energy and environmental policy goals.

The study finally briefly examines a number of tax policy issues to be addressed as governments turn increasingly to energy taxes as policy tools. These include careful definition of terms and goals relating to internalisation, tax neutrality, and harmonisation; questions of infrastructure; the appropriateness of taxing energy as a proxy for pollution; and the appropriateness of using energy taxes versus other instruments as solutions for local and global problems.

INTRODUCTION

Governments tax energy to raise revenues, largely because energy is convenient to tax, and because demand is relatively inelastic, permitting the raising of revenues without significantly eroding the tax base. More recently, taxing energy consumption has gained considerable currency as a possible means to achieve environmental objectives.

Using energy taxes to influence energy consumption patterns is fairly straightforward. Using energy taxes as a tool and a proxy for pollution control, however, requires the balance of fiscal, industrial, competitive, environmental and energy policies.

The levy of energy taxes for whatever purpose cannot be done in a vacuum. Nor can governments expect easy dove-tailing of policy objectives. This study is an attempt to highlight some of the considerations and difficulties that must be faced in designing and implementing energy taxes for other than energy or fiscal purposes.

Energy-related tax levels and tax structures in different OECD countries are likely to elicit different responses to policy actions, including actions intended to harmonise tax levels. Part I of the study therefore begins by examining five case studies of OECD countries with different tax regimes, energy mixes and pollution burdens. The countries selected are Australia, Denmark, Germany, Japan and the United States.

Part II explores the energy tax regimes of these selected OECD countries to discover how adaptable present energy tax regimes might be to new policy applications. Energy taxes are specifically examined for their applicability in the context of fiscal, energy and environmental policies of particular interest to IEA/OECD member countries.

Part III explores considerations to be weighed in deciding to use energy taxes to implement non-fiscal or even non-energy policies, and how such taxes compare to other compliance/incentive mechanisms. Issues addressed in Part III include (i) appropriate internalisation of energy-related pollution costs; (ii) the question of tax neutrality; (iii) the appropriateness of using energy as a proxy for pollution; and (iv) appropriate occasions for harmonisation and relevance to competition .

The study is of limited purpose and scope. It is intended to provide a snapshot of energy taxes, and does not permit correlation between energy taxes and consumption over time. It is not a treatise on taxation or tax reform, nor does it offer quantitative or macro-economic analysis of the effects of change in energy tax policy. The study draws no policy conclusion, and offers no policy recommendations but it does raise important, current questions and suggests pertinent avenues of exploration.

PART I
CASE STUDIES

INTRODUCTION TO PART I

This section presents, without analysis, a catalog of energy-related taxes in five OECD countries, along with a snapshot of energy production and consumption, and a brief look at selected energy-related pollution levels. The facts and figures provided herein, while instructive, are relevant primarily as background to the primary interest of this study, which is to examine those fiscal measures affecting energy prices or costs, and hence the propensity to produce or consume energy. Readers less interested in detailed background might prefer to turn immediately to the comparisons and discussions in Parts II and III.

These case study countries were chosen in part to illustrate the diversity among OECD countries in taxes and in energy needs which affect and reflect different policy objectives. Such diversity must be kept in mind when comparing national tax, energy and environment-related policies and when discussing the possibilities for international policy coordination in these fields.

The taxes described herein include those touching both energy consumption (hence the inclusion of fees, earmarked taxes and motor vehicle taxes), and those which, along with subsidies, affect energy producers. In this latter context, producer income taxes are discussed even though they are not uniquely energy-related, because in some countries energy tax preferences (beyond normal allowances for ordinary business expenses) are administered through the income tax system. However, such tax allowances for energy-related activities are not compared here with those granted to other industries. Also included in some of the cases described below are measures such as producer fees and royalties, which are not taxes. They are included as relevant and for comparison in cases where governments are using both royalties and taxes interchangeably to capture rent.

Most energy taxes have been conceived of and levied as excise taxes for the purpose of raising revenues, either for general revenues or earmarked for specific purposes. Some, though, have also been designed to serve ancillary policies: to capture rents (PRRT in Australia); to redistribute income (German and Japanese taxes that fund coal subsidies); or to encourage changes in consumption (excise differentials on leaded and unleaded gasoline).

This study ultimately tries to make some distinction between energy taxes levied primarily for raising revenue and those levied primarily as incentives to change behaviour in the furtherance of policy goals. The reader should bear in mind, however, that no tax is purely revenue raising or purely an incentive tax. A tax levied to raise revenues is likely to affect price and hence demand, while a tax levied to change behaviour generally does so by affecting prices and hence raising revenues. The existence of this continuum may facilitate the use or adaptation of existing taxes to further a number of newly important policy goals.

One must not, however, impute false policy motives to governments for existing taxes. Much of the evolution of energy taxation has been haphazard. Energy taxes have by and large been enacted individually and largely without regard for other existing taxes or other perhaps conflicting policy considerations. The idea of a coherent energy tax policy coordinated with other energy or environmental policies is still nascent and under discussion.

A. AUSTRALIA

ENERGY TAX PROFILE

Taxes on energy consumption in Australia at the Commonwealth level consist primarily of excise taxes on some petroleum products. Australia does not have a VAT or a general consumption tax.

Commonwealth measures that affect energy producers include a resource rent tax, excise taxes on some crude oil production, and commonwealth royalties. Coal export duties and an excise tax to fund coal research and development were abolished in July 1992.

At the state level, gasoline and automotive diesel are subject to state government business franchise fees (equivalent to excises), imposed mainly on petroleum products wholesalers, depending on the state. Energy producers are subject to some state royalties.

A number of tax credits and tax exemptions or special tax considerations are granted to mining activities including energy producers. Some of these apply to other business enterprises, but may have a special application to, or impact on, the energy sector.

Some special depreciation and write-off allowances are available for mining activities, including the energy producing industries; tax deductibility is granted for certain environmentally engendered costs such as mine site rehabilitation. Moreover, mining, as with other productive activities, qualifies for sales tax exemption on production inputs. Mining is also defined in the sales tax system to cover activities relating to petroleum and natural gas, and specifically to include quarrying, exploring or prospecting, and the restoration and rehabilitation of the mine site.

Commonwealth taxes

Consumption-related taxes

Excise taxes in energy consumption

A distinction peculiar to Australia needs to be made at the outset between excise taxes on consumption of energy, including those on refined petroleum products, and the excise taxes collected by the Commonwealth on certain oil and gas production according to location, vintage and value of output. The former are comparable to consumption-based excise taxes in the other case study countries, and have a direct effect on final energy prices. The latter are more in the nature of producer taxes, and are discussed in that sense below. Excise taxes levied on producers do not necessarily alter final prices since, for example, crude oil is sold directly in competition with overseas crudes that are not subject to the same excise tax. In such cases, the producer excise tax is borne largely by producers as reduced profits.

The Commonwealth Government levies consumption-based excise taxes on most liquid refined petroleum products regardless of country of origin. Certain alternative fuels, such as natural gas and liquid petroleum gas, are excise-free, as are petroleum-based products intended for non-fuel use, such as solvents and lubricating oils. Excise taxes on aviation turbine fuel have been replaced by a user charge on air transport movements.

Customs duties on imported products are set equal to the relevant excise taxes and are collected by the Customs authorities on products as they leave bonded storage in refineries or seaboard terminals. Excise or customs duties are passed through to the consumer in the price of the product. Excise and customs duty rates for refined petroleum products are adjusted each February and August in line with half-yearly Consumer Price Index movements. As a result of low inflation in Australia, the last adjustment was in February 1992, when the excise rates established were:

Excise Taxes - A$ 1992/litre

Motor fuel and diesel	0.2615
Aviation gasoline	0.2538
Fuel oil, heating oil and kerosene	0.05425

There are two exceptions to the broad application of the excise tax on diesel fuel. First, the excise includes a non-specified "road-use" component. Certain non-road users of diesel, with the notable exception of the railroads, are thus allowed rebates on diesel excises. Such rebates are available under the Commonwealth Diesel Fuel Rebate Scheme (DFRS) for forestry and commercial fishing and mining operations (except for vehicles used on public roads); and for residential use including hospitals, aged persons homes and nursing homes. The rebates range from 100 per cent for primary production to 76 per cent for residential users, and are paid on application from users meeting the eligibility criteria. The DFRS replaced an exemption certificate scheme that allowed certain off-road users of diesel fuel to purchase diesel fuel without payment of the diesel fuel excise. For fiscal year 1991/92, the DFRS cost the Treasury some A$ 485.3 million in rebates to mining and the energy sector, and A$ 408.1 million in rebates to agriculture.

Second, a portion of the diesel excise tax is collected from heavy road transport vehicles (over 4.5 tonnes) as an attributable cost recovery charge for vehicle operators' use of the road system. The road user charge, adjusted by the National Road Transport Commission to conform with national road system costs attributable to heavy vehicles and according to their diesel fuel consumption, is currently determined at A$ 0.18/litre. Revenue from this road use portion of the diesel fuel excise is not, however, earmarked to roads.

The excise on aviation gasoline (AVGAS) is largely (more than 90 per cent) appropriated to the Civil Aviation Authority as a contribution towards recovery of the costs of airport navigation, rescue and fire fighting services and other facilities. The AVGAS excise was reduced by 1 cent/litre on 7 May 1992 and further reductions in the order of 2 38 cents/litre should occur in 1992/93, pursuant to the Commonwealth's decision to withdraw from operating local civil airports not administered by the Federal Airports Corporation (FAC). From 1 July, 1988, the comparable excise on aviation turbine fuel was replaced with direct user charges, which apply to air transport movements at major Australian airports administered by the FAC.

Commonwealth excise taxes on coal of A$ 0.25/tonne were abolished in July 1992. The larger A$ 0.2 portion of this tax, used to fund the coal industry long service leave scheme on a pay-as-you-go basis, has been replaced and continued under a new and fully funded scheme. The A$ 0.05 of the tax, used to fund government-managed coal-related R & D efforts, has been dropped because research efforts have been assumed in full by industry. An export duty of A$ 3.50 for high quality coking coal from certain open cut mines, initially introduced as a form of windfall profits tax, was also abolished in July 1992.

In fiscal year 1990/91, federal revenues from these customs duties and excise taxes on energy amounted to A$ 6.6 billion, including customs duties of A$ 4.3 million on petrol, A$ 1.5 million on diesel and A$ 25.4 on fuel oil. Total energy excise duties accounted for about 7 per cent of tax receipts in that year.

Most of this excise revenue comes from motor fuel taxes. In 1988/89, for example, the last year for which a breakdown of excise taxes was available, excises on motor fuels (petrol and diesel) amounted to some A$ 3.7 billion and A$ 1.5 billion respectively, or 6 per cent of total Commonwealth tax revenues for that fiscal year.

By contrast, in fiscal year 1981/82 total federal revenues from energy-consumption related excise taxes (petroleum products excise taxes and coal export duties) amounted to A$ 1.1 billion and contributed less than 3 per cent to total federal tax receipts.

Motor vehicle taxes

While motor vehicle taxes are not energy taxes, they have an indirect relationship to the cost and propensity for using motor fuels. As such they are of interest here. Motor vehicle taxes are levied at both the Commonwealth and state levels, and are broadly defined here to include registration fees and licenses.

The Commonwealth levies a wholesale sales tax on motor vehicles, and tariffs on imported motor vehicles. As of 1 January 1992, tariffs on imported motor vehicles applied at the rates of 35 per cent for passenger motor vehicles and 15 per cent for commercial vehicles. Tariffs on passenger motor vehicles are to be reduced at the rate of 2.5 percentage points per year starting in 1993, to an ultimate level of 15 per cent in 2000.

Sales taxes are applied to the wholesale value of new motor vehicles at various rates depending on the type and value of the vehicle. A rate of 15 per cent applies to sub-luxury passenger motor vehicles, 20 per cent for commercial vehicles and 30 per cent for luxury passenger motor vehicles (motor cars, station wagons and 4 wheel drive vehicles retailing above A$ 17,000, a threshold subject to annual indexation). In 1990/91 sales tax revenues from motor vehicles amounted to A$ 1.4 billion, some 16 per cent of total sales tax revenues for that year. Sales taxes are also levied on tyres, batteries, oil and greases, parts and accessories.

Taxes on energy production

Australia is a major energy producer, and energy production comprises a significant share of the country's GDP. Revenues from energy production are important. Taxes levied on energy producers thus represent a fine balance between the government's need to capture a share of the rents and the revenue generated by energy production, and the need to encourage continued investment and growth in the energy sector.

Income taxes

Energy producers, like other private businesses, are subject to Commonwealth company income taxes at the general rate of 39 per cent, applied as a flat rate on assessable income remaining after allowable deductions. Special deductions for mining companies (including oil, gas and coal) are related primarily to exploration and capital expenditures and are not unlike those for energy producers in other OECD countries.

Capital expenditures incurred in mining operations for the purpose of obtaining, among others, oil and gas and coal, including spending on buildings and improvements necessary to the oil and gas operation, are deductible as ordinary business expenses on a straight-line basis over the lesser of ten years or the life of the project. Eligible expenditures include acquisition of prospecting rights, cash bids paid for offshore permits or production licenses, construction expenditures for mine-site employee housing and provision of services on, and access to, the mining site, and LNG liquefaction plant construction expenditures incurred before May 1988. However, capital expenditure on plant and equipment used in mining activities (e.g., mining machinery) must be depreciated under the general depreciation provisions, which since February 1992 have allowed acceleration beyond effective life.

Capital expenditures on facilities used to transport the products of general mining, including coal mining, petroleum and quarrying operations away from the site of those operations, such as road, railway, pipeline or port facilities, are deductible on a straight line basis in equal installments over ten years. There are also some sales tax exemptions for pipeline construction.

Capital expenditures for exploration are deductible immediately rather than capitalized and written off over time. Mine site rehabilitation expenditures including those for the removal of offshore platforms are also immediately deductible. Plant and equipment used in rehabilitation, however, like all plant and equipment used for production or other purposes, qualifies only for normal depreciation. Both exploration expenditures and special deductions for certain capital expenditures are deductible by the taxpayer from income derived from any source, with taxpayers under certain circumstances able to group and transfer internally their income and deductions.

There are also special deductions for environmental costs and for pollution control. Rehabilitation expenditures qualify for immediate expensing where mining, including petroleum production, is conducted on site, or where exploration takes place. Expenditures beyond mere restoration are excluded. Plant and equipment and capital expenditure on housing and welfare are depreciable under separate provisions of the Income Tax Act. As in most countries and for most industries, recurrent expenditure on pollution control is immediately deductible; capital expenditure in Australia is depreciable over 10 years or the life of the project.

Special taxes

"Excise tax" on crude oil and gas production

Until 1977 oil prices and production volumes were set by Commonwealth regulation, with an import parity pricing scheme tied to a system of allocating local production to local refineries. Import parity pricing was largely achieved through an excise tax on domestic petroleum production. Pricing and volume restrictions were ended in 1977 and the petroleum market completely deregulated in 1988. The Commonwealth still maintains a petroleum production excise tax, but at a fixed rate and regardless of world price.

This excise tax is applicable to both onshore and offshore production of crude oil, condensate marketed with crude oil, and liquified petroleum gas (LPG). The excise tax is a sales revenue based tax computed from a schedule of sales that vary according to the region of production, the annual production levels from the region and the vintage of the project from which the production takes place.

While a number of vintages exist for calculating the levy ("old" oil, "intermediate grade" oil and "new" oil), all excise currently paid in Australia is levied under the "new" oil scale. This scale offers the lowest rates of excise, with the first 8.6 thousand barrels per day of production being excise free, rising to a maximum excise charge of 35 per cent for all production in excess of 13.8 thousand barrels per day. In order to stimulate exploration and development in regions covered by the scope of excise, the first 30 million barrels of crude oil production from onshore fields and new offshore developments are excise free.

Because the excise base is narrowly defined, application of the tax is currently limited to the North West Shelf project (offshore) and ancillary areas. Production from the Bass Strait, the largest producing area, is exempt from excise by virtue of being subject to the Petroleum Resource Rent Tax as described below. In fiscal year 1990/91, gross revenues from the production excise tax were A$ 1.35 billion. It should be noted, however, that these excise taxes are deductible from Commonwealth royalty payments and income taxes, so net revenues to the Treasury would be less than the sum of gross revenues shown for these items.

Condensate when marketed jointly with crude oil is also subject to crude oil excise. At present, no condensate production in Australia is subject to an excise liability. All liquefied petroleum gas and natural gas production in Australia is excise free.

Petroleum resource rent tax

The Commonwealth Petroleum Resource Rent Tax (PRRT) was designed to replace the petroleum excise tax in areas under Commonwealth jurisdiction (i.e., offshore). Designed as a secondary, profits-based tax, the PRRT is considered less inhibiting to investment and production than the sales revenue-related crude oil excise tax. The PRRT also replaces Commonwealth royalty payments.

Producing areas subject to PRRT may include ancillary facilities necessary to production and initial storage of the first marketable commodity, but not facilities for adding value or manufacturing activities further downstream (i.e., not for gas liquefaction or oil refining). In principle, the PRRT could be applied to all production under Commonwealth jurisdiction, but at present it effectively applies only to Bass Strait production.

The PRRT is set at 40 per cent of the excess of net assessable receipts of a project over deductible expenditures, with full deductibility for all of a company's offshore-Australia exploration expenditures (for exploration in areas covered by the PRRT) incurred after 1 July 1990. All other project expenditures are also deductible including those for project development, operation and closing down. Expenditures for restoration work associated with closing down — platform removal and environmental restoration — are deductible in the year incurred, with refunds available from previous years' tax payments where expenditures exceed current year receipts.

Undeducted exploration expenditures incurred after 1 July 1990 are transferable to other PRRT-liable projects. Undeducted expenditures are eligible for annual compounding for future deduction against assessable receipts. General expenditures incurred up to five years before the licence was granted are eligible for compounding at 5 percentage points above the long-term Commonwealth bond rate (LTBR), with exploration expenditures eligible for compounding at 15 percentage points above LTBR. Expenditures incurred more than five years before licensing are eligible only for compounding at a rate that compensates for inflation. Financing costs, private overriding royalty payments, income and fringe benefits tax payments, cash bidding payments and certain indirect administrative costs are not deductible for calculating the PRRT. But PRRT payments are deductible for income tax purposes.

In fiscal year 1990/91, net receipts to the Commonwealth treasury from the PRRT amounted to some A$ 293 million vs. A$ 1.35 billion from the crude oil excise tax. Note that this was the transition year for the extension of PRRT to Bass Strait. As part of the transition, producers paid excise and royalty on crude oil and LPG production and received refunds as appropriate to reconcile the difference between their new PRRT liability and what would have been paid under the old arrangements. PRRT revenues in years since have been much higher: A$ 876 million in FY 1991/92, and an estimated A$ 1.2 billion in FY 1992/93.

Uranium levies

A Commonwealth levy is applied to all exports of uranium concentrate produced in the Alligator Rivers Region of the Northern Territory, which includes the Ranger uranium mine and the former Nabarlek uranium mine. The levy is currently set at A$ 1.30 per kilogram of U308, collected at point of export. The levy is imposed to defray costs borne by the Commonwealth in environmental monitoring and research in the area. It generated revenue of A$ 7.2 million in FY 1990/91, and A$ 4.51 million in FY 1991/92.

A Commonwealth levy - essentially a user fee - is also imposed per kilo of uranium oxide produced, to pay three quarters of the costs of the Office of Supervising Scientist, to monitor the environmental impact of the Ranger uranium mine. The remaining 25 per cent is a direct Commonwealth contribution.

Royalties

Royalties are not taxes. They are payments made to the owner of a resource by a non-owner developer of that resource. Where governments retain ownership of mineral resources, royalties constitute payment by private firms to the government for the profitable use of assets belonging to the public.

However, as noted in the Introduction to Part I, the way in which royalties are calculated and collected can have an impact on incentives to invest or produce energy. Moreover, since governments can also use taxes to collect rents, including royalties in a discussion of taxes on production can be instructive for comparative purposes. In Australia particularly, both excise and profit-based taxes are used interchangeably with royalties to collect rent on energy production.

Royalties are collected on all liquid or gaseous petroleum produced in Australia. The Commonwealth receives royalties on production from offshore areas beyond the three-mile territorial sea, except from Bass Strait where production is subject only to PRRT. Royalties are levied at a rate of between 10 and 12.5 per cent of the wellhead value. The wellhead value is calculated by subtracting from the sales receipts all costs incurred in transporting, processing and storing the petroleum between the wellhead and the point of sale. Any crude oil excise levied on production is deductible in the calculation of royalty.

Royalty receipts collected on the offshore North West Shelf project are shared with the State of Western Australia. The State's normal share is 40 per cent, though special arrangements may also apply. Some Commonwealth gas royalties from the North West Shelf are ceded to the State of Western Australia, and ultimately and effectively transferred to the North West Coastal and Gas Pipeline Authority. These arrangements were made in recognition of take or pay contracts tied to changing gas prices.

Reporting of Commonwealth royalty receipts is complicated by a recalculation and reclassification of royalty payments in FY 1990/91. A minimum of A$ 29 million and a maximum of A$ 337 million are applicable for that year. In either case, total receipts from royalties is far less than from the crude oil excise or the PRRT. Revenues from all three

The Commonwealth Government has retained ownership of uranium in the Northern Territory, and collects royalty-type payments on uranium in the Territory on behalf of and for reimbursement to others. The royalty type payments collected from the Ranger uranium mine comprise:

- 4.25 per cent of gross sales proceeds, less certain specified deductions (principally transportation costs to markets), for disbursement to the Aboriginal Benefits Trust Account;

- 1.25 per cent of gross sales proceeds, less certain specified deductions (principally transportation costs to markets), for disbursement to the Northern Territory Government; and

- A$ 2,000,000 per annum for disbursement to the Northern Lands Council pursuant to an agreement under the Aboriginal Land Rights (NT) Act 1976.

Payments collected by the Commonwealth on uranium sales from the Ranger mine and from the former Nabarlek mine in recent years, and the disbursement of these funds is shown below:

Fiscal year	A $ million Collected and Disbursed to :		
	Aboriginal Benefits Trust Account	NT Government	Northern Lands Council
1990/91	10.41	3.42	2.0
1991/92	6.7	2.08	2.0

Subsidies

In the past few years Australia has revised and simplified its taxes including those on energy. A number of subsidies have been eliminated, but many remain. The Commonwealth provides assistance for the development of mining and energy through grants and subsidies, direct project involvement and the supply of services. Assistance is aimed at improving efficiency and competitiveness.

involvement and the supply of services. Assistance is aimed at improving efficiency and competitiveness.

Commonwealth budget outlays for assistance to the energy industries are shown in the following table. In addition to the sums shown, some programmes also entail state contributions and contributions by industry through levies on production.

Budget Outlays on Assistance to Energy Industries
(A$ million)

Specific Industries	1991-92 Actual	1992-93 Budget
Coal	16.1	10.0
Petroleum and Gas	63.7	3.3
Electricity	8.0	-39.1
Sub-total	87.8	-25.1
General Assistance Diesel Fuel Rebate Scheme (including all mining)	485.3	522.1
Energy Research and Conservation	16.5	21.2
Other General Assistance (including all mining)	69.7	70.2
Sub-total	571.5	613.4
Total	659.3	588.3

Commonwealth outlays in energy research and conservation involve primarily funding for the development and use of efficient energy sources, technologies and practices, and the demonstration of renewable energy technologies. The focus of these research efforts is commercialisation. In addition to these direct government outlays, an investment tax credit of 125 per cent is available for investment in R&D, including for alternative energy technologies and for investments in energy efficiency.

Summary of energy-related revenues

In FY 1990/91, energy-consumption taxes (A$ 6.6 billion) accounted for some 7 per cent of tax revenue. The share of all energy-related consumption taxes (including motor vehicle taxes of A$ 1.4 billion)) was 8.6 per cent of total taxes. Total Commonwealth energy based revenues including energy consumption related taxes, producer taxes other than income taxes, and royalties or rent recovery, amounted to a little over A$ 9.7 billion, or around 10 per cent of total tax and non-tax revenues.

Government expenditures on specific energy industries amounted to some A$ 88 million in that same year.

In fiscal year 1981/82, by contrast, total Commonwealth energy-related revenues were A$ 4.3 billion, with energy-related taxes (including crude oil excises) amounting approximately 11 per cent of total .

State taxes

Consumption-related taxes

Franchise fees on energy consumption

The Australian Constitution precludes states from levying excise lows. Instead, state governments impose business franchise fees calculated on the basis of total sales in a one or six month period, the rates thus changing frequently. Energy consumption is effectively taxed by state governments by the pass-through of these business franchise fees.

State petroleum franchise fees are collected on motor fuel in all states except Queensland. However, off-road use of diesel is generally exempt from the fuel franchise license fees except in Tasmania. Rates as of 1 October 1992 (in A$/litre) for these taxes were as follows:

	Super Leaded Motor Spirit	Regular Unleaded Motor Spirit	Premium Unleaded Motor Spirit	Diesel
NSW	6.86	6.86	6.86	6.90
Victoria	7.46	7.46	8.05	7.17
Queensland	nil	nil	nil	nil
Western Australia	5.67	5.67	5.67	7.45
South Australia	8.94	8.79	8.79	10.03
Tasmania	6.15	6.15	6.15	6.11
NT	6.00	6.00	6.00	6.00
ACT	6.53	6.53	6.53	6.57

Total revenues (in millions of A$) collected by the states and territories from these fuel franchise license fees in FY 1991/92 were as follows:

NSW	VIC	QLD	WA	SA	TAS	NT	ACT
446	372	0	131	86	45	22	23

Motor vehicle taxes and charges

The states and territories also levy charges and taxes on the use of goods and the performance of activities, including those related to motor vehicles and their use. Relevant fees collected on motor vehicles include a stamp duty on the transfer of motor vehicle ownership, and annual registration fees for motor vehicles ranging from A$ 500 to A$ 940 (which includes a third party accident insurance premium). Revenues from these two charges in 1991 are shown in the Table below:

Revenue from stamp duty on vehicles (A$m)

NSW	VIC	QLD	WA	SA	TAS	NT	ACT
176	196.3	84.3	75.3	61.3	21.7	n.a.	9.3

Revenue from motor vehicle registration fees (A$m)

NSW	VIC	QLD	WA	SA	TAS	NT	ACT
713	229.1	373.5	87.7	118.8	20.9	10.6	37.5

Royalties from energy production

The states do not tax oil and gas production. However, they do collect rent on the production of minerals they own. Royalties on oil and gas production are paid to state governments for production from fields within the territorial sea and in the state/territory jurisdiction onshore. State royalty rates are 10-12.5 per cent of wellhead value, identical to the Commonwealth rates. States may alternatively levy a resource rent royalty (RRR), or may levy any other type of tax on onshore oil and gas developments within their jurisdiction.

The RRR is similar to the Commonwealth's PRRT that operates in offshore areas, with some minor differences with respect to the deductibility of exploration expenditure and the application of the long term bond rate to development expenditures. Where the producers and the state enter into an RRR agreement, and the Commonwealth and state enter into a revenue sharing agreement, Commonwealth crude oil excise taxes and state royalties can be replaced by the RRR. At present, the Barrow Island project in Western Australia is the only project specifically covered by the provisions of RRR. However, the Northern Territory has a profit-based royalty somewhat analogous to and operating roughly in the same way as the Commonwealth PRRT.

Coal producers are subject to royalties in both principal black coal producing states: Queensland and New South Wales. (Western Australia and Tasmania also produce some black coal; Victoria and Southern Australia produce sub-bituminous coal and lignite).

Queensland levies a royalty of 4-5 per cent of the freight value of the coal for underground and open cut coal respectively, along with a A$ 0.05/tonne royalty on coal used within Queensland. In New South Wales, coal producers pay a royalty of A$ 1.70/tonne, plus an additional A$ 0.50/saleable tonne from certain open cut mines, imposed initially as a form of windfall profit tax in 1982. New South Wales also levies an excise tax on coal to fund restoration of homes damaged by mine subsidence.

In addition to these overt charges, both Queensland and New South Wales have used government monopoly power over railroad rates to capture some of the rents from each coal mining operation or expansion in their respective jurisdictions. Both states charge what are known as excess freight rates for shipping coal, i.e. rates above the cost of transport. Each individual mining license is negotiated as a package including production rights, possible contributions to state infrastructure, and freight rates, resulting in a wide variation and distortion of costs. Negotiated royalties and freight rates are set by the states based on estimated profitability of each mine, but freight rates unlike royalties, do not fluctuate as clearly with coal prices.

The excess component in freight rates in Queensland has been estimated to vary from a low of A$ 4/tonne to a high of A$ 8/tonne; in New South Wales the range of estimates is A$ 1-5/tonne. It is unclear whether New South Wales in fact still collects substantial rents through excess freight rates; there is little doubt that Queensland does so. Queensland collects an estimated A$ 300-500 million annually from excess freight rates.

The South Australia State Government collects royalty from the Olympic Dam copper/gold/silver/uranium project at the rate of 2.5 per cent of gross sales revenue (at mine gate). The royalty rate is scheduled to increase to 3.5 per cent in 1993. In addition there is provision for payment of profit related royalties once a threshold rate of return is reached.

ENERGY PROFILE[1]

Australia is a major producer of all fuels and an exporter of coal, uranium and natural gas. Over the past decade, the government has made major reforms in the structure and the regulatory and fiscal framework of the energy industries. It has simplified taxation, reduced price controls, subsidies and government ownership, generally creating a more market-based energy sector.

The changes in energy supply from 1979-1990 and the composition of total primary energy supply (TPES)[2] in 1990 are shown respectively in Figures 1 and 2.

Figure 1: **Total TPES and TPES by Fuel in Australia, 1979 and 1990**

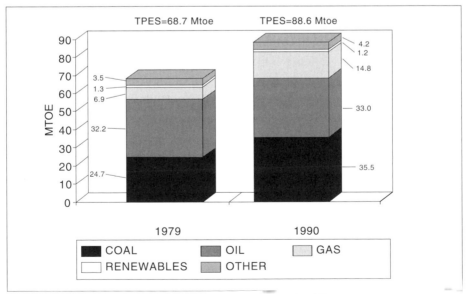

1. The figures in ....mun are taken from *IEA statistics Energy Policies of IEA Countries, 1991 Review,* and do not necessarily conform to national statistics by virtue of differences in definitions, estimation and/or measurement. IEA figures have been used in the case studies whenever possible, for purposes of comparibility.
2. Total primary energy supply comprises all energy (domestic production and imports) available to an economy for transformation and for final consumption. In IEA energy balances TPES has replaced its analog Total Primary Energy Requirement (TPER) as the measure of energy consumed.

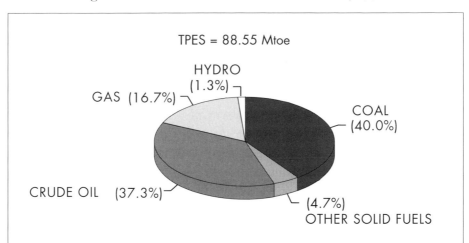

Figure 2: **Fuel Shares in TPES in Australia, 1990**

TPES = 88.55 Mtoe

HYDRO (1.3%)

GAS (16.7%)

COAL (40.0%)

CRUDE OIL (37.3%)

(4.7%) OTHER SOLID FUELS

Oil is the only primary fuel in which Australia is not an exporter; domestic crude oil production accounted for some 89 per cent of domestic crude supplies in 1990. LNG exports began in 1989 and in 1990 amounted to 2.4 Mtoe, or 14 percent of domestic production. Coal exports for the year amounted to some two-thirds (68 Mtoe) of total coal output.

Australia is a major uranium producer and exporter; 4388 metric tons of U308 were produced in 1990/91 and 7218 metric tons were exported, including stocks from the now closed Nabarlek mine, stocks of uranium produced as a by-product from gold mines, and from current production. Australia has no nuclear power sector of its own, so virtually all uranium mined is either stocked or exported. Stock build up and drawdown are thus important adjuncts to uranium production and marketing.

Electricity generation has grown steadily since 1979 from 7.8 Mtoe to 13.2 Mtoe in 1990. The generation mix for 1990 is shown in Figure 3. Coal is by far the dominant fuel, and the electricity sector is the major domestic market for coal, accounting for some 75 per cent of domestic black coal consumption and consuming virtually all brown coal produced.

Figure 3: **Fuel Shares in Electricity Output in Australia, 1990**

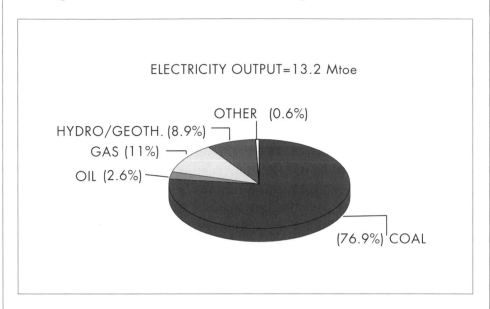

ELECTRICITY OUTPUT=13.2 Mtoe

OTHER (0.6%)

HYDRO/GEOTH. (8.9%)

GAS (11%)

OIL (2.6%)

(76.9%) COAL

The changes in total final consumption between 1979 and 1990 and the fuel mix for total final consumption in 1990 are shown respectively in Figures 4 and 5. Final consumption by sector is shown in Figure 6. Note that final consumption of coal is small (only 4 Mtoe), since most coal is consumed in the transformation sector. The transformation sector also consumes almost half of total natural gas output. Final consumption of electricity is fairly evenly divided between industry, and the residential and commercial sector (roughly 5 Mtoe each in 1990).

Figure 4: **Total TFC and TFC by Fuel in Australia, 1979 and 1990**

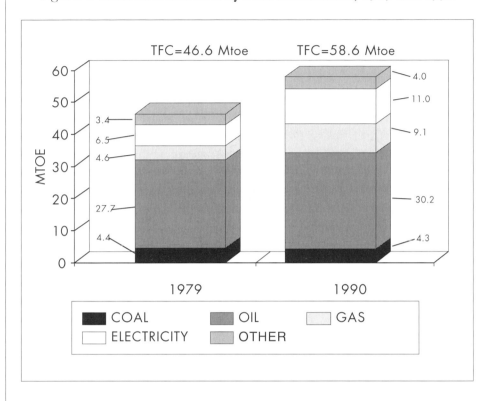

Figure 5: **Fuel Shares in TFC in Australia, 1990**

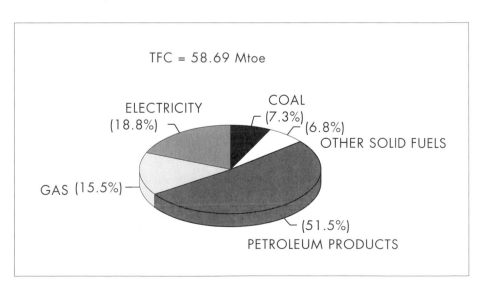

Figure 6: **TFC by Sector in Australia 1990**

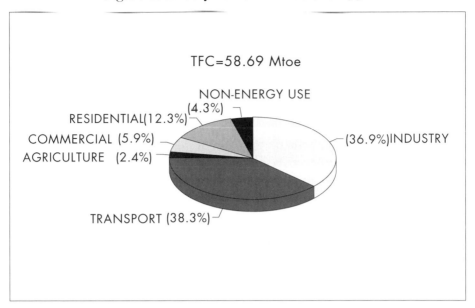

TFC=58.69 Mtoe

NON-ENERGY USE (4.3%)

RESIDENTIAL(12.3%)

COMMERCIAL (5.9%)

AGRICULTURE (2.4%)

(36.9%)INDUSTRY

TRANSPORT (38.3%)

ENERGY-RELATED POLLUTION PROFILE[3]

Coordinated national data as compiled by the OECD on energy-related pollution in Australia are limited to CO_2 emissions. Emissions data for SO_2 and NO_x are available only for major urban areas and only for 1983. National statistics on particulates are available only for mobile sources and only for 1987-88. One cannot therefore discuss improvements or deterioration. Moreover, measurements of emissions as compiled by the Australian government may not be comparable with the OECD data used for other case study countries. Nevertheless, the figures available have been included here to provide some indication of energy-related pollution in Australia. The cities for which SO_2 and NO_x figures are available include: Adelaide, Brisbane, Canberra, Darwin, Hobart, Melbourne, Perth and Sydney.

CO_2 emissions

CO_2 emissions in Australia, primarily (75 per cent) from stationary sources, grew from a total of 221 million tons in 1980 to 274 million tons in 1990. The relative contributions to emissions by various sectors in 1990 are as follows: electricity generation, 128 million tons (47 per cent of total emissions); oil refineries, 4.1 million tons; other industries (including agriculture and mining), 45.5 million tons; residential and commercial, 8.3 million tons. In 1980, by comparison, electricity generated

---

3. The statistics for CO_2 used in these Energy-Related Pollution Profiles have been compiled and calculated by the IEA/OECD as current but as yet unpublished updates of the statistics in the *OECD Environmental Data Compendium 1991*, and may not correspond exactly with national statistics. The statistics on other pollutants in Australia are taken from state and Commonwealth sources. Because of differences in definition and/or measurement, they may not be comparable to those used in the other case studies, which are taken (unless otherwise indicated) from the *Compendium*..

88 million tons of CO_2 (40 per cent of total emissions); oil refineries, 9.3 million tons; other industries, 45.5 million tons; residential and commercial, 8.2 million tons.

Mobile source emissions grew from 55 million tons of CO_2 in 1980 to 67.7 million tons in 1990, but still accounted for a steady 25 per cent of total CO_2 emissions in both years.

In 1988, emissions of CO_2 per unit of GDP amounted to 404 kg/US\$ 1 000 (1985), and per capita amounted to 4.3 kg/cap. In that same year the OECD averages for these ratios were 286 kg/US\$ 1 000 (1985) and 3.4 kg/cap.

SO_2 emissions

Sulfur dioxide emissions result primarily from fossil fuel combustion and vary with the sulfur content of the fuel. These emissions are a principal contributor to acid rain and other forms of acidification of the environment, along with nitrogen oxides. In general, Australian domestic coal is low in sulfur; flue gas desulfurisation is therefore not considered necessary and the technology is not installed in power plants or other stationary sources.

Energy-related SO_2 emissions in the eight major cities in 1985 amounted to some 80 kt, 8.8 kt from mobile sources and 71 kt from stationary sources. Of these latter, the transformation sector accounted for almost half the emissions: 27 kt from power generation, primarily in Brisbane and Adelaide; and 28.4 kt from petroleum refineries, primarily in Sydney, Perth and Melbourne. Industry accounts for the remainder.

On average, mobile sources account for 11 per cent of total energy-related SO_2 emissions, though the range varies greatly among states and territories, from 79 per cent in Canberra, where there is virtually no industry, to 2 per cent in Darwin where power generation accounts for 98 per cent of SO_2 emissions.

NO_x emissions

Man-made nitrogen oxide emissions are primarily energy-related, stemming from fossil fuel combustion and arising mostly in the transport sector. These emissions contribute to photochemical smog and, along with sulfur dioxide, to acid rain and other acidification of the environment.

Energy-related nitrogen oxide emissions in the eight major cities in 1985 amounted to some 261 kt, the greatest bulk (77 per cent) coming from mobile sources. Eleven per cent is attributable to power generation.

Particulates

Unchecked emissions of particulates in the energy sector are largely related to coal and oil use and are highly susceptible to pollution control efforts.

Particulates emissions in Australia in 1987-88 attributable to mobile sources were estimated to be some 20 kt.

B. DENMARK

ENERGY TAX PROFILE

Denmark has made serious efforts to influence fuel use and mix through high and differentiated taxes on fuels and energy uses, including rebates and subsidies. A new tax structure has recently been implemented that is designed to achieve and balance a number of policy objectives and social goals, including the evolution of energy consumption patterns which the government deems environmentally desirable.

The Danish tax system is characterized by high rates for both income and consumption. The corporate tax rate is 34 per cent; personal income tax rates range from 50-68 per cent. Two thirds of total revenue comes from income taxes and one third from consumption taxes and excise duties, a ratio that has been stable for many years. More than half of consumption taxes come from VAT, the other half from excise taxes, primarily on motor vehicles, energy, tobacco and alcohol.

Current taxes on energy consumption in Denmark include the VAT; excise taxes on oil products, coal and electricity; special taxes consisting primarily of storage fees for oil products; and two taxes on motor vehicles, on registration and on weight, which might be considered to affect fuel use.

As for taxes on energy production, there is a tax levied on hydrocarbon production and on those whose income is derived from the extraction of hydrocarbons in Denmark. There are also provisions relating to energy production and consumption in the corporate tax code. Royalties, though not taxes, are collected from energy producers and are included here for comparison with the rent capturing aspects of the hydrocarbon tax.

Energy taxes were formerly used to stabilise energy prices at 1985 levels. This practice was discontinued after the 1989 energy tax reform, but its effects can still be seen in the relatively higher taxes for oil vs. coal, reflecting taxes geared to evening out fluctuating oil prices at a time of relatively stable coal prices.

Energy subsidies exist in the form of exemptions from energy taxes for renewable energy production and for some combined heat and power (CHP) producers (for the energy they use to generate electricity but not for energy they use to generate heat). Some technologies are also subsidised.

VAT

The general tax rate for the VAT in Denmark is now 25 per cent, highest of the case study countries. The VAT is refunded in full for all commercial purposes except gasoline consumption, which is subject to the full VAT rate. All private energy consumption is subject to full VAT.

Denmark is unique among the case study countries in that it grants rebates on energy-related excise taxes to consumers eligible for VAT rebates. Those not eligible for rebates, or those who pay no VAT, must pay excise taxes. Rebates are provided instead of exemptions to facilitate collection and monitoring. Since taxes are paid and rebated on the initiative of the taxpayer, the incentive for reporting is high. Both excise duties and VAT must be clearly marked on all relevant bills including energy bills. Both kinds of taxes are collected through the VAT system and rebates may be collected by netting out payments due and owing.

Excise taxes on energy consumption

All energy excise taxes in Denmark except for gasoline taxes are now defined as having two components: an "energy" component and a "CO_2" component. The first is akin to the standard excise tax; the latter is a form of carbon-based tax set roughly, with some exceptions, to vary with the carbon content of various fuels. The tax rates are thus different for each fuel. Non-energy uses are not taxed.

The administration of these excise taxes (collection, exemptions, rebates) varies according to consumer, with households subject to the full excise tax, businesses eligible for partial exemptions, and energy intensive industries eligible for full rebates.

For purposes of simplicity and comparability, all energy excise taxes are discussed below simply as straightforward excise taxes, with a single total tax level given for each fuel, as in the other case studies. The details of the carbon-based tax scheme, and the breakdown of the different fuel-related tax rates, are discussed separately in the section on Special Taxes.

Motor fuel excises

The excise duty on gasoline is now set at Danish Kroner (DKr) 2.9/litre for leaded gasoline and DKr 2.25/litre for unleaded (now more than 70 per cent of consumption). The tax is levied on all gasoline and blends, payable on delivery from a registered business (i.e. producers, importers or wholesalers of the taxable goods), or effectively within two months of delivery. Gasoline used for agricultural tractors, stationary motors, fishing vessels and aircraft (and for defense purposes until January 1993), is exempt from the tax. These uses amount to less than 1 per cent of total consumption.

A special fee is also levied on gasoline sold by companies participating in Denmark's strategic emergency petroleum storage program (TDO). In theory, the tax is applicable to all oil products and constitutes a compulsory storage fee to pay for the maintenance of the TDO stocks. The fees have varied by product and over time. As of now, automotive diesel, light oil and heavy fuel oil are no longer assessed for the compulsory storage fee. The levy is applied only to gasoline at a rate of DKr 0.008/litre.

The excise tax levied on motor diesel fuel applies to diesel used in all motors: vehicles and stationary motors including on- and off-road motor uses of construction and mining equipment; and agricultural uses, (except aircraft and ships, including fishing vessels). Non-motor uses of diesel and household uses such as heating, are taxed at a different rate from motor diesel. They are subject instead to the same excise duties listed below for other oil products.

The motor fuel diesel tax is DKr 2.04/litre for normal diesel and a reduced rate of DKr 1.98/litre for "clean" diesel fuel. Clean diesel is defined by characteristics which produce low particulates emissions in combustion. The principal feature is a low (0.05 per cent) sulfur content (vs. 0.2 per cent for normal diesel). Clean diesel combustion emits some 10 per cent fewer particulates than normal diesel and some 75 per cent less SO_2. There is also a scarce, very light diesel, generally reserved for public buses, which has some 30 per cent lower particulates emissions than normal diesel. Buses and public transport using clean or ultra light diesel are given a rebate of DKr 0.3/litre, including VAT. A rebate of DKr 0.55/litre is also granted for buses using LPG, which produces even fewer particulates than ultra light diesel.

Excise taxes on other fuels

Excise duties on other petroleum products are as follows:

Fuel	Tax Rate
Gas oil, light fuel oil and kerosene for heating	DKr 1.76/litre
Heavy fuel oil	DKr 1.98/kg

All taxes are payable when the fuel leaves the manufacturer or wholesaler. Rebates or partial rebates of these excise taxes are available to commercial users eligible for VAT rebates. Households and non-registered VAT payers are liable for the whole tax.

Natural gas is not taxed though gas prices are tied to the prices, including taxes, of competing fuels. The consumer arguably perceives no effective difference in final price than if natural gas were taxed, except that the tax is not transparent, and the gas companies are subsidised by being permitted to collect this implicit tax for their own benefit.

LPG used as motor fuel is subject to tax of DKr 1.24. The tax is DKr 2.3/kg for LPG used as bottled gas for non-motor uses. The tax is payable upon delivery of the gas from a registered producer. Businesses eligible for VAT refunds are also eligible for refunds of the excise tax on LPG.

Coal and lignite (including briquettes) and coke are subject to excise taxes of DKr 932/ton for coal and coke and DKr 683/ton for lignite. The tax is payable when coal is delivered or consumed by registered businesses or imported by non-registered businesses. A registered business is one which mines or produces coal (required to register with the customs service); businesses with a coal storage capacity of more than 1 000 tons and which sell, store or consume coal may also register themselves, effectively becoming bonded warehouses and so exempt from the tax on the use of coal within their premises.

Coal used to produce electricity or gas, however, is exempt. Businesses eligible for VAT refunds are also eligible for a full refund of the excise tax on the coal they consume, except not businesses that supply heating.

In the case of electricity generators, for CHP and for district heating, the excise scheme is somewhat more complex. Fuel for electricity generated and sold by power stations and combined heat and power stations, is exempt from excise taxes. Instead, electricity consumers pay a tax on the electricity they buy, calculated on the basis as if all power had been generated using coal, with some standard average heat content and at some standard average generating efficiency, and assuming normal excise tax had been paid on the coal.

This provision is particularly important given Denmark's sometimes relatively large and widely fluctuating power trade with other Scandinavian countries and with Germany. Input taxes on domestically used generating fuels would be passed on in exports as an average tax, which is sufficient for domestic purposes but not for international trading regulations to which Denmark is bound. These regulations require a precise calculation of local duties to assure perfect correlation of rebates on exports and levies on imports. Failure to do so can be considered subsidisation of exports. To avoid this problem, Denmark taxes electricity output, the tax being collected from final consumers in their bills. Electricity exports are exempt from the tax and imports subject to the uniform electricity tax.

The excise tax is due on all electricity consumed in Denmark, except that businesses eligible for VAT refund are also eligible for refund of the excise tax. The tax is due from the producer when the power is delivered to the consumer. However, electricity produced exclusively for the producer's own consumption from small (less than 150 KW) plants, from emergency generators or on board vehicles, is exempt from the tax.

Excise taxes on electricity vary slightly with consumption levels and according to end use. Households with electric heat pay a low rate on the first 4000 KWh/year consumed, on the presumption that this is for heating. All consumption over 4000 KWh/year, and all homes without electric heat pay a higher rate presumptively for other-than-heating. The lower heating rate is DKr 0.335/KWh; the higher non-heating rate is DKr 0.37/KWh.

Fuel used for district heating plants, however, or for generating heat in CHP plants, is not exempt from energy excise duties. Moreover, CHP producers are not permitted to deduct the energy component of these excise taxes on the heat they sell, even though as registered VAT companies they would otherwise be eligible for such rebates. CHP and DH plants must pay excise taxes on fuel for heating, but are allowed to pass on the energy tax in their bills for heat. Commercial customers eligible for VAT and excise tax refunds may then obtain rebates for this tax as part of their own regularisation.

Revenues from energy excise taxes in 1990 amounted to DKr 5.6 billion for petrol and DKr 8.7 billion for all other fuels. This amounts to some 3.6 per cent of total tax revenues in that year.

Special taxes

As of May 1992, a tax of DKr 100/ton of CO_2 (about US$ 16/ton of CO_2) was imposed in principle on all private household energy consumption. Although labelled as a CO_2 tax, i.e. a tax on emissions, the tax is actually levied as a tax on carbon-based fuels used as inputs to combustion. Tax rates for the different fuels roughly correspond to relative carbon content, with some adjustments. The rates imposed for each fuel are as follows:

Fuel	Tax Rate
Gas oil (light fuel oil and diesel oil)	DKr 0.27/l
Fuel oil	DKr 0.32/kg
Coal	DKr 242/t
Electricity	DKr 0.1/kWh

No carbon tax is levied on natural gas.

Previous energy excise taxes were adjusted to accommodate these new taxes. The net result of this reform process is that taxes on electricity (for households) and coal have been somewhat reduced but not by as much as the level of the carbon-based tax: the net increase for electricity for households was DKr 0.04/KWh, and DKr 167/ton for coal. Total taxes for households on oil and gas remain unchanged.

Industrial and commercial energy users will be subject to this tax as of 1 January 1993. However, companies eligible for VAT and for energy excise tax refunds can also receive an immediate refund of half the tax (i.e., DKr 50/ton of CO_2). Companies may also subsequently be refunded all or part of the rest of the carbon-based tax, depending on the ratio of their carbon-based tax liability to their net VAT liability, calculated for these purposes as the net of sales (less exports) minus purchases subject to VAT. The part of the carbon-based tax that exceeds 1 per cent of this calculated VAT base can be refunded 50 per cent; the part that exceeds 2 per cent receives a 75 per cent refund; everything over 3 per cent receives a 90 per cent rebate.

Energy intensive enterprises may reduce the CO_2 tax even further up to a limit of 100 per cent (except for a minimum required payment of DKr 10,000 per year). The more energy intensive the industry, the higher the rebate, which can provide perverse disincentives for energy efficiency and undermine the presumed goal of the tax, namely to reduce fossil energy consumption and thereby reduce CO_2 emissions. Issues surrounding the question of exempting energy intensive and other industries from energy and carbon-based taxes, are discussed in Part III.

Although no carbon-based tax is levied on natural gas, a complex gas subsidy/pricing scheme, devised as an accompaniment to the carbon-based tax, attempts to provide incentives for using natural gas in electricity generation while imposing a shadow tax on it. Small, local CHP companies using gas for electricity consumption buy gas from the national distributor at the price of oil, less the relevant energy tax. Gas for district heating is sold at the price of oil plus the relevant energy tax. The incentive for the gas company has thus been to sell gas for heating. Under the new adjustment scheme, gas prices for CHP electricity generation have been raised by an amount more or less equivalent to an imputed carbon-based tax, but with the gas company pocketing the revenue, and increasing the incentive to sell gas for CHP electricity generation.

At the same time, small-scale gas-fired CHP power generation, along with renewable energy based electricity producers, receives a subsidy of DKr 0.1/KWh. This subsidy is not passed on to electricity consumers. This scheme is intended to send corrective marginal cost signals to electricity producers and consumers; the cost of choosing gas is reduced to generators, but the price of electricity, most of which is still generated from coal, remains high to consumers.

The government anticipates net revenues of some DKr 2 billion per annum from these carbon-based "CO_2" taxes, half of which is expected to come from electricity consumption. Half of these revenues will be used to subsidise energy conservation and district heating and half will be used to reduce other taxes.

Motor vehicle taxes

There are two excise taxes on motor vehicles. One is levied at registration, and varies from 125-180 per cent of the vehicle purchase price (including VAT, but excluding excise taxes) for passenger cars, and from 20 to 95 per cent of the price for caravans and commercial vehicles. Some two thirds of the price of a registered car in Denmark is tax. For an average priced car of about DKr 170 000, DKr 100 000 is tax, including VAT. Reduced rates are offered to commercial vehicles or vehicles with special safety features or pollution control equipment.

The other motor vehicle tax is levied on all registerable vehicles according to weight. The tax rate ranges from DKr 452/year for motorcycles to DKr 2260/year for vehicles weighing 800-1000 kg, to DKr 5 424/year for vehicles weighing 2001 kg and over, with an additional DKr 301/kg of own weight over 2001 kg. The tax on hauling vehicles (vans and lorries), is calculated inversely on the basis of total permitted weight; other vehicles are taxed on the basis of own weight; some few vehicles have a flat fee. Defense, emergency and public bus vehicles are exempt from the tax, as are taxis, mopeds and vehicles for invalids. Passenger vehicles equipped to burn diesel must also pay an equalisation tax in addition to the weight tax to compensate for the fact that the gasoline tax is higher than the diesel tax.

There is a third vehicle-related excise tax on liability insurance for drivers, used to fund third party liability insurance.

While these vehicle excise taxes are not directly related to energy, the high tax on private vehicle registration and the progressive tax on private vehicle weight provide incentives for having fewer cars, and using smaller, more fuel efficient, private vehicles. On the other hand, both registration and weight taxes on commercial vehicles are levied in inverse proportion to size, and so create perverse incentives to build larger sized commercial fleets.

In 1981 revenues from vehicle excise taxes amounted to some DKr 6.4 billion, or 3.3 per cent of total revenues. In 1990 the total was DKr 13.2 billion, 3.4 per cent of total revenues.

Since 1980, the relative share of revenues from energy related consumption taxes (as shown in *Taxes and Excise Duties,* 1991, Danmarks Statistik) has changed as follows:

Tax receipts in billion DKr	1981	1990
Total tax receipts to national government	127.0	261.0
Motor vehicle excise taxes	6.4	13.2
Registration	3.2	7.9
Weight	2.8	4.3
Insurance	0.4	0.9
Petrol duty	3.6	5.6
Other energy excise taxes	3.3	8.7
Total energy-related excise taxes	13.3	27.5
As per cent of total revenue	10.4	10.5

Production-related taxes

Hydrocarbon tax

The hydrocarbon tax was devised as a form of windfall profits tax on oil and gas production in Denmark. Although the conditions and calculations governing payment of the hydrocarbon tax are complex, a company essentially pays only a hydrocarbon tax when corporate profits due to oil price changes and related to hydrocarbon production exceed 25 per cent of the company's investment in oil and gas. Under these conditions, the hydrocarbon tax is paid on profits above the 25 per cent threshold.

The hydrocarbon tax is designed as a supplement to the personal or corporate income tax due and payable for each resident or nonresident person or company deriving income from or in connection with the extraction of hydrocarbon in Denmark. Such persons or corporations must calculate their hydrocarbon income separately from other income. The latter is taxed according to general rules, while special income tax rules as well as the hydrocarbon tax apply to the former.

The general hydrocarbon tax rate is 70 per cent. The general corporate tax rate is 38 per cent or 34 per cent, depending on the time of payment. For hydrocarbon industry employees not liable for Danish income tax, there is a hydrocarbon tax rate of 30 per cent on gross income and without deductions. This provision is not used.

Special rules for calculating taxable hydrocarbon income include full deductibility for exploration expenses, and extended loss carry forward of 15 years (versus 5 years for regular income tax). Production plant, platforms, pipelines and other income earning equipment are depreciated according to normal rules for working plant. A special investment allowance equal to 25 per cent of the investment in a field is granted annually for ten years, including the year in which depreciation of the asset began. Hydrocarbon taxes are calculated on a field-by-field basis. Income cannot be averaged between and among fields, except that losses in abandoned fields can be deducted from the total taxable hydrocarbon income from profitable fields before the tax is calculated.

Personal and corporate income tax payable on income from hydrocarbon extraction under the regular personal and corporate income tax laws, is wholly deductible from the total personal or corporate income calculated as subject to the hydrocarbon tax in the same year.

Revenues have been collected under the hydrocarbon tax since 1984. In the intervening years revenues have varied from a low of DKr 17 million in 1989 to a high of DKr 966 million in 1987. Revenues in 1984 and 1990 respectively were DKr 38 million and DKr 486 million.

Royalties

Royalties are not taxes, and in Denmark they are being replaced in part by the hydrocarbon tax as a means of capturing rents. Nevertheless, royalties do contribute to energy-related government revenues and so are included here. Licensed oil and gas production are subject to royalties ranging from 2-16 per cent depending on volume, but there is no royalty obligation attached to licenses issued since 1989. Revenues from royalties in 1990 amounted to DKr 633 million.

Subsidies

Subsidies for indigenous energy production consist primarily of subsidies for CHP companies providing district heating. In addition, renewable energy and natural gas are exempted from energy and CO_2-related taxes. The consequence of this tax exemption is an improvement of the natural gas companies' financial situation on the order of DKr 1.8 billion a year. There are no comparable figures available for renewable energy.

Direct subsidies to renewable energy sources besides R&D funding amounted to DKr 525 million in the period 1986-89, of which DKr 197 million went to wind energy, DKr 103 million to biomass, and DKr 84 million to solar energy. No updated figures are available. Direct subsidies given to CHP and energy conservation have been about DKr 600 million a year.

ENERGY PROFILE[1]

Denmark produces domestically more than half (55 per cent in 1990) of its total primary energy supply (TPES), largely from North Sea oil and gas, but also including some small contribution from renewable sources. In the field of oil and gas, self-sufficiency is even higher. In 1990, domestic production of some 6.1 Mtoe and 2.8 Mtoe respectively accounted for 85 per cent of TPES for these two fuels. Renewable energy amounted to about 1 Mtoe in 1990 or about 5.7 per cent of TPES. Denmark has no indigenous coal production. Some 6.25 Mtoe p.a. of coal is imported, mostly for use in power production and for CHP plants.

Denmark's growing domestic energy production amounted to some 9.93 Mtoe out of 18.2 Mtoe in 1990. Total final consumption by contrast was 14 Mtoe, the difference being largely due to generation losses and net imports of electricity. The changes in Denmark's energy supply for the period 1979 to 1990 can be seen in Figure 1. Figure 2 shows the total primary energy supply mix for 1990.

Oil and gas output are expected to rise through the turn of the century. Gas has been part of the Danish energy economy only since 1984, yet domestic gas production already accounted for 15 per cent of TPES in 1990. The excess of domestic gas production over consumption permits exports to Sweden and to Germany. The Government has been making a concerted effort to encourage greater use of gas for a number of reasons, including environmental concerns.

Generation of electricity in Denmark has risen steadily to 2.2 Mtoe in 1990. A sometimes large and variable part of Danish electricity supply is traded internationally on the NORDEL and UCPTE grids with Norway and Sweden (depending on hydropower production in these countries) and

---

1. The figures in this section are taken from *IEA statistics Energy Policies of IEA Countries, 1991 Review*, and do not necessarily conform to national statistics by virtue of differences in definitions, estimation and/or measurement. IEA figures have been used in the case studies whenever possible, for purposes of comparibility.

with some exports to Germany. Net imports have moved from zero in 1985-86 to a peak of 9.5 TWh in 1989 (32 per cent of national electricity consumption). Net imports for 1990 were much lower again, at 0.6 Mtoe (7 000 GWh). In 1991 and 1992 Denmark was a net exporter of electricity.

Figure 1: **Total TPES and TPES by Fuel in Denmark, 1979 and 1990**

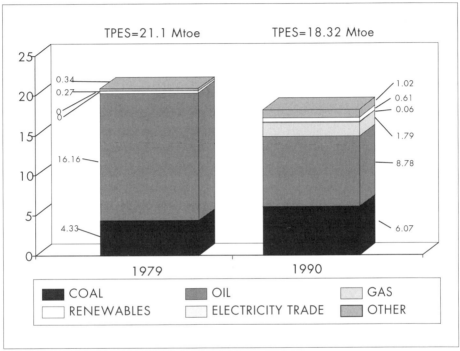

Figure 2: **Fuel shares in TPES in Denmark, 1990**

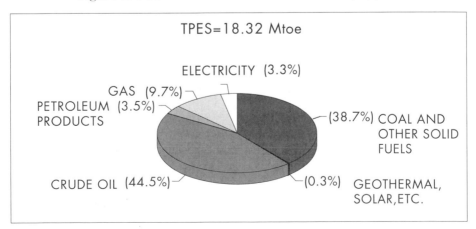

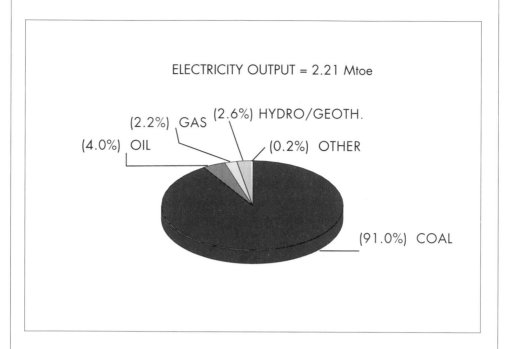

ELECTRICITY OUTPUT = 2.21 Mtoe

(2.2%) GAS   (2.6%) HYDRO/GEOTH.

(4.0%) OIL   (0.2%) OTHER

(91.0%) COAL

The fuel mix for domestic electricity generation is shown in Figure 3. Coal, virtually all imported, is the dominant fuel, accounting for over 90 per cent of generating fuel requirements. Plans for increased use of gas and biomass are geared to reducing the use of coal by the end of the century. Some 50 per cent of coal-fired power generation is now provided by CHP, a share that is expected to grow.

CHP and district heating occupy a rather important place in the Danish energy delivery system. Most CHP is coal-fired in central generating stations. These plants in 1990 accounted for about 60 per cent of district heating in Denmark. a share expected to rise. Small existing district heating plants are also converting into CHP plants. These small district heating plants are now largely fuelled by gas. The government plans to encourage use of biomass.

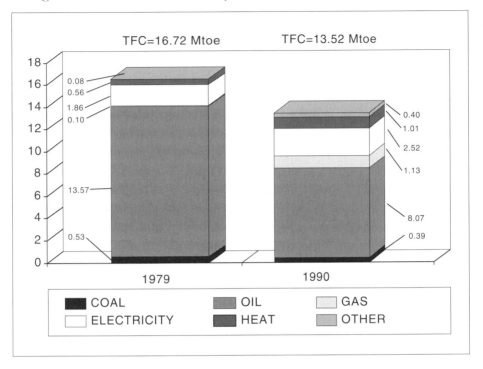

Figure 4: **Total TFC and TFC by fuel in Denmark, 1979 and 1990**

Figure 5: **Fuel shares in TFC in Denmark, 1990**

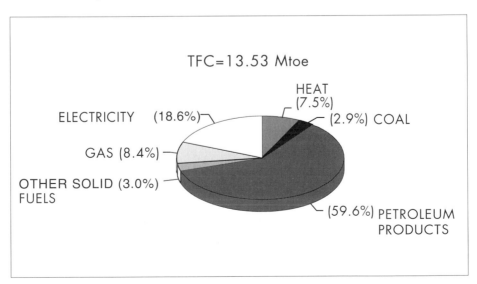

Changes in final consumption from 1979 to 1990, and the fuel and energy mix for final consumption in 1990 are shown in Figures 4 and 5 respectively. Figure 6 shows final consumption by sector. Since 1979, and outside of the transport sector, oil's share of the energy mix has declined steadily. In 1979, oil accounted for 60 per cent of TFC; by 1990 oil had fallen to 52 per cent, including a growing transport sector.

Figure 6: **TFC by sector in Denmark 1990**

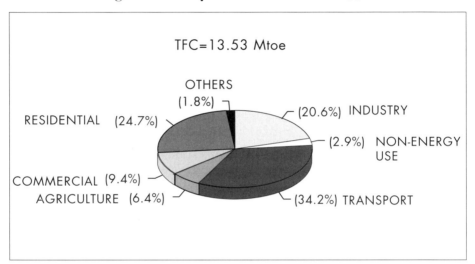

ENERGY-RELATED POLLUTION PROFILE[2]

Energy-related pollution in Denmark stems primarily from fuel combustion in two sectors: domestic transport and electric power/process heat production. The primary pollutants stemming from this include CO_2, SO_2, NO_x, and particulates. One could expect stationary-source pollution to decline as more gas is substituted for coal in generating plants, but automobile-related pollution is likely to increase with a growing car stock and increased vehicle use.

CO_2 emissions

Annual energy-related CO_2 emissions in Denmark have actually fallen from 63.9 million tons of CO_2 in 1980 to 56.3 million in 1990. Some of this reflects changes in net imports of electricity from Sweden and Norway. As noted earlier, these imports can be an important part of the TPES in Denmark in a given year. Danish CO_2 emissions will always be lower to the extent that imported electricity replaces domestic generation, assuming present capacity with the current fuel mix highly concentrated on coal. Since electricity in Sweden and Norway is generated by nuclear (Sweden) and hydro power, global emissions are also reduced when Denmark imports power from these countries.

Almost half (45 per cent) of these emissions come from the electricity generation and refining sectors (25.2 million tons in 1990), with industry boiler use accounting for another 5.6 million, and residential and com-

---

2. The statistics for CO_2 used these Energy-Related Pollution Profiles haves been compiled and calculated by the IEA/OECD as current but as yet unpublished updates of the statistics in the OECD *Environmental Compendium 1991*, and may not correspond exactly with national statisics. The statistics on other polluants in Denmark are taken from the *Compendium* and may not correspond with national statistics.

mercial energy users contributing 6 million tons of CO_2 annually. Total emissions from stationary sources in 1990 were 39.4 million tons of CO_2, 70 per cent of the total. Mobile sources contributed 16.9 million tons of CO_2 in that year.

In 1980, by comparison, electricity generation and refineries emitted 26.6 million tons of CO_2 (42 per cent of total). Other sectoral shares include: industrial boilers, 7.9 million tons; residential and commercial, 15.2 million tons. Total emissions were 63.9 million tons; total stationary source emissions were 51.9 million tons. Mobile sources accounted for 12 million tons in that year, 19 per cent of the total.

The changes in sectoral contributions to emissions over time reflects a number of factors, including gains in energy efficiency. The drop in emissions of CO_2 in the transformation sector despite the dominance of coal in the generating mix and despite a growth in generation, is impressive. Emissions from mobile sources have continued to grow, reflecting growth in the car stock and in vehicle use.

Danish emissions of CO_2 per unit of GDP in 1988 was 294 kg/US$ 1 000 (1985) versus an OECD average of 286 kg/US$ 1 000 (1985) and reflecting a growth in emissions of only 5 per cent from 1971 to 1988. Per capita emissions in 1988 were 3.4 kg/cap., the same as the OECD average.

SO_2 emissions

Sulfur dioxide emissions are directly related to the sulfur content of fossil fuel burned, and/or to the quality and level of sulfur removal from the combustion emissions stream. Total SO_2 emissions in Denmark fell by more than half (from 447 kt to 193 kt) from 1980 to 1989, reflecting primarily a drop in stationary source emissions (from 436 kt to 182 kt) during that period, the result of improved pollution control and of a certain amount of fuel switching. Emissions from mobile sources were the same (11 kt) at the end of the decade as at the beginning, but rising to a high of 15 kt in 1985 and falling to a low of 10 kt in 1986 in the interim.

The decline in stationary source emissions has thus been more dramatic than improvements in mobile sources. The overall improvement in emissions is reflected in a reduction of SO_2 concentrations (micrograms/m³) measured in Copenhagen, from an index figure of 1980 = 100 to 58 in 1989.

Note that a protocol to reduce sulfur dioxide emissions by 30 per cent from 1980 levels by 1993 went into effect in 1987. SO_2 levels even before 1987 were declining, however, reflecting structural changes in the economy, some fuel switching, energy savings and the evolution of pollution control policies and technologies.

By the end of the 1980s, Danish SO_2 emissions had fallen by half despite economic growth. Emissions per unit of GDP by 1989 were 4.1 kg/US$ 1 000 (1985) and per capita emissions 47.2 kg/cap. (OECD averages were 4.1 and 48.3 respectively).

NO_x emissions

The transport sector bears somewhat more responsibility for NO_x than it does for SO_2 emissions. In 1988, total NO_x emissions in Denmark amounted to some 249 kt, of which mobile sources accounted for 89 kt, or some 36 per cent. The remaining 160 kt came from stationary sources.

Emissions of nitrogen oxides rose erratically in Denmark from 241 kt in 1980 to 249 kt in 1988. Some 60-66 per cent of these emissions historically have come from stationary sources. Mobile source emissions, grew almost steadily from 76 kt in 1980 to 89 kt in 1988.

Since 1988 there has been a requirement for catalytic converters, initially only encouraged by tax considerations, to be installed in all new cars. The results of this should be reflected in future emissions levels.

NO_x emissions per unit of GDP in Denmark in 1989 were 4.2 kg/US$ 1 000 (1985); per capita emissions were 48.5 kg/cap., slightly above the OECD average (3.8 kg/US$ 1 000 (1985) and 44.3 kg/cap. respectively) in both cases.

Despite variable growth in emissions over time, concentrations (micrograms/m³) of NO_x measured in Denmark (in Copenhagen) reflect a considerable improvement from an index base figure of 100 in 1982 to 66 in 1989. Such improvement stands in marked contrast to increased concentrations over the base year (1980) in selected cities in the United States (especially Denver) and in Germany (Berlin and Frankfurt).

Particulates

The energy sector is generally the major cause of particulates emissions, arising from combustion of fossil fuels. Unfortunately, data are available only on particulates emissions from mobile sources in Denmark, and on concentrations. Since 1980, mobile source emissions have risen from 3 kt to 4 kt per annum. In most other countries, particulates emissions from mobile sources comprise only a small portion of total particulate emissions. There is no reason to suspect the same is not true for Denmark.

Limited data indicate that concentrations (micrograms/m^3) of particulates in Copenhagen grew from a base figure of 100 in 1982 to 139 in 1989, which might suggest rise in total emissions as well. Given the heavy use of coal for electricity generation, and the growth in the electricity sector, such an increase might be expected.

C. GERMANY

ENERGY TAX PROFILE

Under the Unification Treaty, the five new Länder formerly comprising the GDR were essentially brought under the legal, fiscal and institutional structure of the Federal Republic. Most of these adjustments will be phased in. This study focuses on the present unified fiscal regime, recognising that a description of the tax system prevailing in the new Länder before unification could perhaps shed more light on energy use and pollution trends in those regions since 1980.

Taxes in Germany that touch energy consumption include the VAT, excise taxes, and, special taxes. Income taxes and subsidies affect primarily energy producers. Energy savers also benefit from special or reduced income tax rates and some subsidies. Since Germany has a federal system of government, Länder as well as the national government may levy taxes, but within the context of the federal tax legislation. Länder also levy royalties on crude oil and natural gas production.

Federal taxes

Consumption-related taxes

VAT, or turnover tax

Among national taxes, the VAT is levied at the general rate of 15 per cent of the ex-tax value of a product or service, on gasoline, light fuel oil used by households, electricity for households, and natural gas used in households. As in most European countries, the VAT is refunded at 100 per cent for all purchases for commercial purposes. This means that no VAT is collected for industry uses of energy, for energy used in electricity generation or on automotive diesel.

The VAT is levied on imports at point of entry and is deducted for exports. The benefits of the VAT are divided between the federal government (65 per cent) and the Länder governments (35 per cent). In 1991, the revenues from VAT amounted to DM 180 billion, of which the revenues from energy-related VAT accounted for DM 4.84 billion.

Excise taxes

Energy excise taxes are levied primarily on petroleum products (called mineral oils), at the following rates:

Excise taxes on petroleum products
DM/1992

Fuel	Tax
Gasoline	
Leaded	0.92/litre
Unleaded	0.82/litre
Automotive diesel	0.54/litre
Aviation fuel	0.57-0.67/litre
Light fuel oil	
For households, low lead	0.137/litre
high lead	0.15/litre
For industry, low lead	0.08/litre
high lead	0.093/litre
Heavy oils	
For lubricating and cleansing	532.5/t
For heating, gas oils	68.5/t
For heat generation	30/t
For electricity generation	55/t

All mineral oil excise taxes are the responsibility of the refiner/importer but are at least partly passed through to the final consumer at the point of retail sale. Taxes are payable on all mineral oils and similar products manufactured in or imported into taxable areas (i.e. not foreign customs enclaves or custom-free zones). The duty is payable when goods leave the manufacturing enterprise or are withdrawn for consumption within the enterprise (other than for daily operating purposes). Enterprises, for purposes of taxation, can also include bonded warehouses, including warehouses for imports and exports. Mineral oils used other than for motor fuels, lubricants or for heating can be exempt from the tax under certain circumstances, as can certain exports.

The most important excise tax is levied on gasoline. The excise rates favour unleaded over leaded gasoline, with the sale of leaded regular gasoline having been banned in western Germany since 1987. In 1990 revenues from this tax amounted to some DM 30 billion.

Excise taxes on heavy fuel oils vary greatly from the standard rate (primarily for lubricating and cleansing oils) of DM 0.5325/ton. The tax on heavy oil is used largely as a lever for reducing coal subsidy expenditures, since the maintenance price for coal is tied to the price of heavy oil. Higher excise taxes raise the final price of heavy oil, thus reducing the differential to be subsidised. In 1990, revenue from this tax amounted to some DM 200 million.

Natural gas (and other non-liquid gaseous hydrocarbons), when used for heating, is subject to an excise tax of DM 0.36/100 KWh.

In 1980 in the old Länder, energy-related tax receipts amounted to some DM 21.34 billion or 5.9 per cent of federal revenues. The relative share of taxes in the final price of various fuels amounted on average to some 56 per cent.

The total collected from these same taxes in Germany in 1990 was DM 36.64 billion, of which DM 31 billion came from taxes on motor fuels. Note that the tax code as applied to the eastern Länder incorporated several variations until 31 December 1990. In 1991, with a uniform regime, total German revenues from energy taxes were DM 47.3 billion, or 7 per cent of total tax receipts (DM 662), of which 33 billion came from taxes on motor fuels.

Motor vehicle taxes

All motor vehicles registered for road use, including motorcycles, are subject to a tax besides VAT based on cylinder capacity or weight.

Rates range from DM 3.6/25 cc for motor cycles; to DM 13.2 - 21.6/100 cc for passenger cars; and DM 22 - 25/200 kg for all other vehicles. There is a surcharge of DM 16.4/100 cc for diesel-fuelled passenger cars to compensate for lower taxes on diesel fuel. In contrast, reduced tariffs are granted for certain types of commercial vehicles, including those over 7000 kg. Rates are intended to reflect at least roughly the pollution capacity of the vehicle. A more direct tax on measured pollutant emissions is being considered to replace the present scheme. The taxes are collected annually or quarterly and the revenues go to the benefit of the Länder.

Special taxes

Special charges are levied on mineral oils primarily to finance national commitments for emergency petroleum storage. These are not always shown as taxes. The rate charged for gasoline is DM 0.0072/litre; for diesel, DM 0.0059/litre; for light fuel oil, DM 8.64/MT; for heavy fuel oil, DM 7.5/MT.

A special tax on electricity (Kohlepfennig) is levied on electricity producers and collected from consumers in their tariffs. Revenues are earmarked as part of a complex scheme (Ausgleichsabgabe) to provide financial support to the western German hard coal industry, and so actually constitute a cross-subsidy. Certain German electricity generators (those party to an agreement called the Jahrhundertvertrag) are required to buy specified quantities of domestic coal at prices that cover the coal producers break-even costs (net of direct subsidies). To partially compensate these generators for this much higher-than-market cost of using domestic coal, the Kohlepfennig is charged to electricity consumers, with exceptions provided for the iron and steel and non-ferrous metal industries (who are therefore themselves partly subsidized by other electricity consumers and generators, while being obliged to buy a certain quota of domestic coal for their own use). Household consumers of electricity must pay a VAT of 14 per cent on the Kohlepfennig levy as well as on their own consumption.

The monies are put into an electricity generation fund (Verstromungsfonds), out of which partial compensation is paid to public power plants according to a complicated formula based in part on world energy prices. The rate of the special tax is set each year by the Minister for Economics, according to estimated needs of the fund. For 1992, the rate is 7.75 per cent of the consumer's electricity tariff, down from a high of 8.5 per cent in 1989. The levy for 1993 is scheduled to be 7.5 per cent. When this rate is insufficient to compensate for the difference in costs for buying domestic versus imported (i.e. world price) coal, the Verstromungsfonds is financed by government credit.

In 1991, the revenues from this Kohlepfennig amounted to some DM 7.6 billion, less exceptions amounting to some DM 60 million in the first half of 1992. The scheme does not apply to the new Länder, and is now scheduled to end in 1995.

Subsidies

State aid to coal production

Besides the electricity-tariff-based coal subsidy scheme, support of the German hard coal industry in the old Länder includes both aid to current production as well as aid to cover outstanding obligations but not directly supporting current production; cross-subsidies among German consumers and Länder; and direct and indirect subsidies from government expenditures. Cross-subsidies are generally effected through the required purchase of domestic coal by the steel and electricity industries, paid for at least in part by steel and electricity consumers, the latter through the Kohlepfennig. Direct government expenditures are numerous and complex. They are generally shared two-thirds by the Federal government and one-third by those Länder with hard coal production. [Note: There is no hard coal production in the new Länder.]

Total financial support includes grants for capital investment (or to cover operating deficits), special depreciation allowances, bonuses to miners working underground; several special financial measures to assist with corporate debt for the two largest companies; price support to cover the difference between production costs and selling price; other support measures include payments for special retirement, early retirement, and redundancy payments, training and relocation aid to miners, special write-off and amortisation of unproductive assets related to restructuring (direct payments for closures under restructuring were stopped in 1986), environmental and R&D aid, funding of coal-based combined heat and power (CHP) and district heating, and maintenance of strategic coal stocks.

The total cost of these measures in 1991 amounted to almost DM 22 billion. The share of these various measures that was used directly or indirectly to aid current production in 1991 amounted to some DM 11.9 billion, or an average of some DM 181/ton domestic German coal. Along with price supports, including refunds through the thermal (electricity) coal levy, and cross-subsidies through additional consumer payments for thermal and coking coal, these measures comprise the producer subsidy equivalent (PSE), a measure used by the OECD to describe and compare the distorting effects of subsidies. The PSE for German hard coal has been rising steadily.

Other subsidies

The Federal Government and the Länder also provide a number of subsidies for energy efficiency improvements including grants for investment to house owners, and a 10 per cent deduction in income tax liability in the new Länder for building modernisation and energy conservation. Some DM 875 million are earmarked for direct grants to fund up to 20 per cent of the cost of energy conservation projects in the eastern Länder; low cost loans are also available.

At the federal level, funding is available for energy conservation for small and medium-size companies for energy-efficient improvements in buildings, and for machines which improve energy efficiency or which use alternative energy sources. The program will pay for up to 50 per cent of the cost of the investment, up to a ceiling of DM 3 million in the old Länder and DM 1 million in the new Länder. Technical assistance and advice on energy savings can also be funded under a federal program (up to 40 per cent of the cost of the consultant fee), with a ceiling of DM 3000-6000 per case.

Länder taxes

Länder may levy special taxes and/or local excise taxes, so long as they do not correspond to those under federal legislation. The Länder collect royalties on energy production at rates which vary from 0 to 40 per cent. Federal income taxes are administered by the Länder pursuant to federal law. The Länder receive 42.5 per cent of the receipts from federal income taxes, as well as 35 per cent of the VAT and 50 per cent of the Körperschaftsteuer (corporate income tax).

Unlike the United States, where states have autonomy to levy and administer taxes, the German tax scheme stems exclusively from federal legislation, with Länder administration of the federal tax in the case of income and corporate taxes. The result is a homogenous tax scheme. The two exceptions to this are royalties, which are completely the domain of the Länder, and municipal authority to apply different rates to a special business tax.

ENERGY PROFILE[1]

The case of Germany is unique, in that unification overnight altered the energy profile of the country. IEA data do not yet reflect historical energy statistics of unified Germany. The figures in this section illustrating historical changes (1979-1990) therefore only reflect energy statistics for the old Länder, which nevertheless account for 85 per cent of total German energy consumption and 86 per cent of total German energy production. Statistics for 1990 for unified Germany are available from the German Bundesministerium für Wirtschaft. Figures dealing only with 1990 data thus reflect both IEA statistics for the old Länder and statistics provided by the German government for unified Germany.

Figure 1 shows the growth in TPES in the old Länder from 1979 to 1990, and TPES for unified Germany for 1990. Figures 2 and 3 show the fuel mix for TPES for unified Germany and for the old Länder respectively for 1990.

Germany produced 43 per cent of its own total energy supply (152 Mtoe out of 353 Mtoe) in 1990. The bulk of this was coal: 50 Mtoe of hard coal and 75 Mtoe of brown coal. Germany is almost self-sufficient in coal, though this is entirely due to the protective measures (price supports, market guarantees, and trade restrictions) in force in the old Länder. Declining hard coal output in the region has been heavily cushioned by increased subsidies.

These subsidies are maintained in part through hard coal import tariff barriers for the old Länder and with the cooperation of the electricity generating-coal mining complex. The new Länder, by contrast, may

---

1 Note that the statistics for unified Germany were provided by the German Bundesministerium für Wirstchaft. Some definitions and some measurements (particulary for nuclear and for hydro) are different from, and the statistics are therefore not entirely comparable with, the IEA energy figures in the other case studies. Statistics relating to the old Länder only, unless otherwise indicated, are taken as for the other case study countries from *Energy Policy in IEA Countries, 1991 Review*.

Figure 1: **Total TPES and TPES by Fuel in Germany, 1979 and 1990**

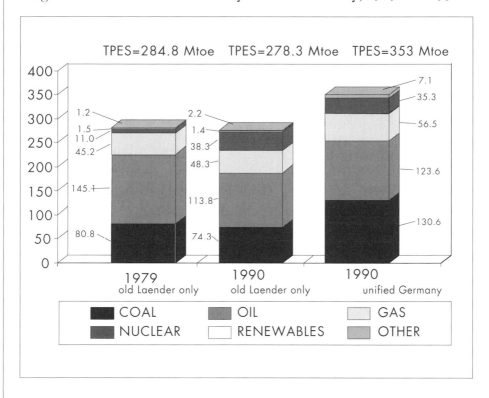

Figure 2: **Fuel shares in TPES in unified Germany, 1990**

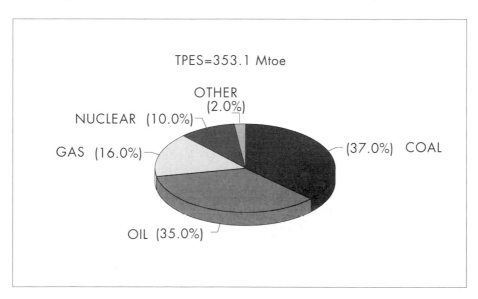

Figure 3: **Fuel shares in TPES in Germany (Old Länder only), 1990**

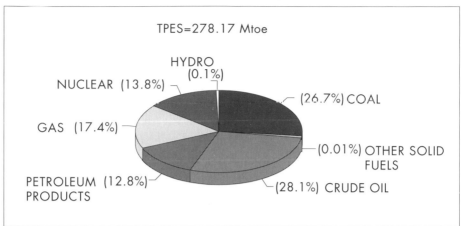

TPES=278.17 Mtoe

HYDRO (0.1%)

NUCLEAR (13.8%)

(26.7%) COAL

GAS (17.4%)

(0.01%) OTHER SOLID FUELS

PETROLEUM (12.8%) PRODUCTS

(28.1%) CRUDE OIL

import coal freely and without restriction. It was assumed that management of east German electricity generation by west German conglomerates would probably sustain the trade restrictions in the new Länder. It is not clear, however, that such partial tariff barriers can be maintained in a unified Germany, particularly where the monopoly of the large mining and generation companies is being challenged by municipal enterprises or large industrial users. There are in fact already plans for generating plants in the new Länder using imported hard coal.

The brown coal (lignite) industry receives no public support despite a dramatic drop in demand and output, particularly in the new Länder since 1989. According to figures provided by the Bundesministerium für Wirtschaft, brown coal production in all of Germany in 1980 was 81 Mtoe, and 75 Mtoe in 1990 (of which 53 Mtoe were from the new Länder). In that decade, production peaked in 1985 at 90 Mtoe (of which 66 Mtoe were from the new Länder). By contrast, brown coal production in the new Länder is expected to fall to 28 Mtoe for 1992.

German figures show that electricity production grew from 41 Mtoe (475 Twh) in all of Germany in 1980, to 47 Mtoe (550 Twh) in unified Germany in 1990. Figures 4 and 5 show the fuel mix for electricity generation for unified Germany and for the old Länder respectively. The dominance of coal is particularly noticeable in the electricity generating sector, though the present mix is expected to change somewhat with a drop in brown-coal-fired generation in the new Länder and an increase in the use of gas.

Figure 4: **Fuel shares in electricity output, unified Germany, 1990**

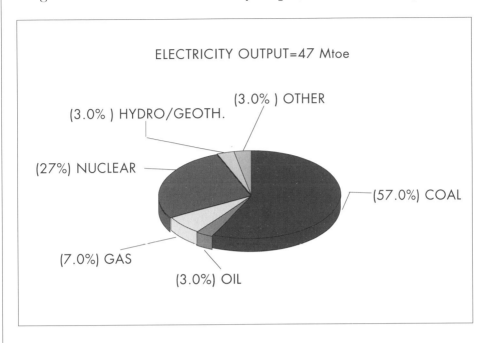

ELECTRICITY OUTPUT=47 Mtoe

(3.0%) OTHER

(3.0%) HYDRO/GEOTH.

(27%) NUCLEAR

(57.0%) COAL

(7.0%) GAS

(3.0%) OIL

Figure 5: **Fuel shares in electricity output in Germany
(old Länder only), 1990**

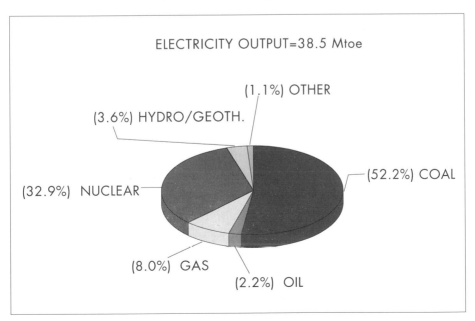

ELECTRICITY OUTPUT=38.5 Mtoe

(1.1%) OTHER

(3.6%) HYDRO/GEOTH.

(32.9%) NUCLEAR

(52.2%) COAL

(8.0%) GAS

(2.2%) OIL

In 1990, electricity generation accounted for more than half of brown coal consumption in the new Länder, about 80 per cent of electricity generation (16 000 out of 20 000 MW) was lignite-fired. Now more than one third of eastern generating capacity is being shut down, with lignite-fired capacity planned for the end of the decade at 10 000 MW.

While coal is clearly the dominant fuel in the German transformation/consumption mix, it plays only a minor role in total final consumption. Fuel shares for final consumption in 1990 are shown in Figures 6 and 7 for unified Germany and for the old Länder respectively. The changes in final consumption, from 1979-90, for the old Länder only, are shown in Figure 8.

Figure 6: **TFC by fuel in unified Germany, 1990**

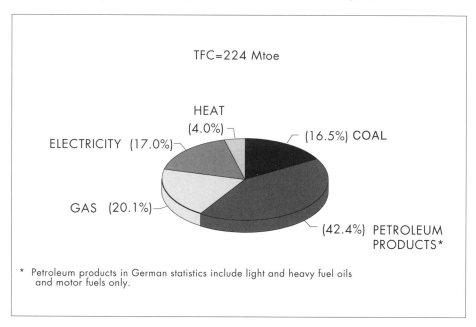

TFC=224 Mtoe

HEAT (4.0%)

ELECTRICITY (17.0%)

GAS (20.1%)

(16.5%) COAL

(42.4%) PETROLEUM PRODUCTS*

* Petroleum products in German statistics include light and heavy fuel oils and motor fuels only.

Total energy consumption in unified Germany is expected to decline slightly in the medium term, particularly during the period of economic adjustment required to absorb unification and to begin economic recovery in the new Länder. Oil, coal and especially brown coal are expected to lose shares in TPES, in TFC and in electricity generation, giving way primarily to natural gas. These trends reflect in part convenience and environmental considerations (substituting gas for coal and oil), cost considerations (for domestic coal), the increasing availability and diversity of natural gas supplies, and increasing oil and energy efficiency, particularly in transport. Any gains in this last area, however, are likely to be swamped by absolute transport growth in the new Länder.

Figure 7: **TFC by fuel in Germany (old Länder only), 1990**

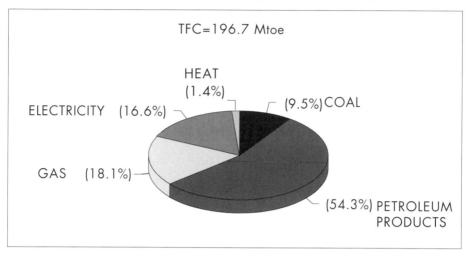

TFC=196.7 Mtoe

HEAT (1.4%)
ELECTRICITY (16.6%)
(9.5%) COAL
GAS (18.1%)
(54.3%) PETROLEUM PRODUCTS

Figure 8: **Total TFC and TFC by Fuel in Germany, 1979 and 1990**

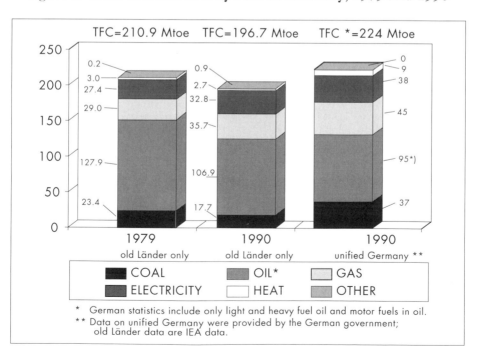

* German statistics include only light and heavy fuel oil and motor fuels in oil.
** Data on unified Germany were provided by the German government; old Länder data are IEA data.

Demand for lignite in the eastern Länder is changing rapidly, reflecting changes in the ownership of power generating companies, in industrial output and in consumer choices. In the short run, consumption of lignite in this region is expected to decline as economic activity, and hence electricity demand, falls. In the longer term the dramatic drop in lignite consumption may well be reinforced as capital turnover permits replacement of existing boilers with ones capable of burning other fuels. Half of the brown coal consumed in the new Lander has traditionally gone to home heating, 25 per cent of which was lignite-fired district heating and 69 per cent briquettes. In 1989, some 50 million tons of briquettes were used in home heating: by 1992, the figure was 9 million tons, expected to fall to 4 by the end of the decade, as consumers are able to choose other fuels.

The same is true for district heating. Although the Federal government and the Länder are each paying DM 150 million to subsidise the preservation and modernisation of DH plants, many of which are coal-fired, municipalities given the choice are opting for oil and gas.

Sectoral shares in final consumption in 1990 are shown in Figures 9 and 10, for unified Germany and for the old Länder respectively.

Figure 9: **TFC by sector in unified Germany, 1990**

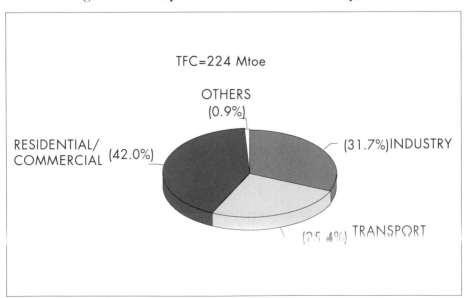

TFC=224 Mtoe

OTHERS
(0.9%)

RESIDENTIAL/
COMMERCIAL (42.0%)

(31.7%)INDUSTRY

(25.4%) TRANSPORT

Figure 10: **TFC by sector in Germany (old Länder only), 1990**

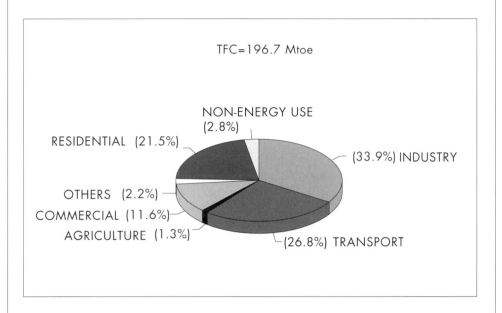

ENERGY-RELATED POLLUTION PROFILE[2]

Energy-related pollution in Germany stems from two main sources: combustion of coal, including and especially brown coal, and transportation. Combustion of coal produces different results in the new and old Länder primarily as a function of coal quality and of air pollution control technologies available or in place. Transport-related pollution also varies between the two regions, in part as a function of pollution control technologies, but also in large part because of differences in engine design and efficiency. The Trabant automobile widely used in the former GDR has a 2-cycle engine with largely uncontrolled emissions.

CO_2 emissions

Emissions of CO_2 in Germany fell from 1980 to 1990, from 1.1 billion tons to 1.0 billion. This drop in total emissions, however, masks a growth in CO_2 emissions in the transport sector from 146 million tons in 1980 to 181 million tons in 1990. Virtually all stationary source sectors showed improvements in emissions levels: industrial emissions dropped from 229 million tons to 126 million tons in the ten year period. These gains were realised despite growth in both industrial output and in electricity generation.

---

2. The statistics for CO_2 used in these Energy-Related Pollution Profiles have been compiled and calculated by the IEA/OECD Secretariat but are not unpublished updates of the statistics in the OECD Environmental Data *Compendium 1991*, and may not correspond exactly with national statistics. The statistics on other pollutants in Germany are taken from sources provided by the Bundesministerium für Wirtschaft. Because of differences in definition and/or measurement, they may not be comparable to those used in the other case studies, which are also taken (unless otherwise indicated) from the *Compendium*. The national figures have been used to include the new Länder in unified German statistics.

OECD-calculated ratios of CO_2 emissions to GDP and to population are only available for the old Länder. For this region only, the OECD figures for these emissions ratios are 294 kg/US$ 1 000 (1985) (vs. an OECD average of 286); and 5.2 kg/cap. (vs. the OECD average of 3.4).

SO_2 emissions

Emissions of SO_2 are a function of the sulfur content of fuels used for combustion, and the availability of desulfurisation technologies. Emissions of energy-related SO_2 in Germany have been reduced dramatically in the last decade. German statistics show such emissions declining from a total of 7.4 million tons in 1980 to 5.6 million tons in 1990, with virtually all improvement occurring in the old Länder; emissions actually grew in the new Länder during the period. This growth in SO_2 emissions in the eastern Länder reflects a growth in energy use, and the complete lack of desulfurisation equipment. Since these Länder account for 85 per cent of all SO_2 emissions in Germany, the potential for improvement with proper equipment is enormous.

Emissions from mobile sources (about 2 percent of total emissions) have fallen from 165 kt to 120 kt, reflecting improvement in all Länder. Stationary source emissions have fallen from 7.3 million tons to 5.5 million.

Reductions in SO_2 emissions are reflected by a drop in measured SO_2 concentrations (micrograms/m³) in selected German cities in the old Länder. Using 1980 as a base year, the index of SO_2 concentrations by 1989 had fallen from 100 to 68 in Berlin (West), and to 38 in Frankfurt and in Gelsenkirchen.

Emissions of SO_2 in western Germany by 1989 as a ratio of west German GDP, amounted to 1.9 kg/US$ 1 000 (1985). Per capita emissions for western Germany in that year were 17.3 kg/cap. The OECD averages for these two ratios are 4.1 kg/US$ 1 000 (1985) and 48.3 kg/cap. respectively.

NO_x emissions

Emissions of NO_x result primarily from the burning of fossil fuels at high temperature. In Germany, NO_x emissions from mobile sources have risen from 1.9 million tons in 1980 to 2.2 million tons in 1990, with all of the increase being in the old Länder and reflecting primarily the growth in the car stock. By contrast, gains in NO_x emissions control at stationary sources have reduced emissions from these sources from 1.6 million tons in 1980 to 1.0 million tons in 1990. Again, virtually all gains have been made in the old Länder. Overall, NO_x emissions have fallen somewhat in the last decade, from a total of 3.5 million tons to 3.2 million tons.

Despite these improvements, concentrations of NO_x (micrograms/m^3) measured in selected German cities have generally increased. Measured against a base year of 1980 = 100, concentrations measured in 1989 had risen to 123 in Berlin (West), 102 in Frankfurt, and had fallen only in Gelsenkirchen, to 60.

Measured as a ratio of GDP (for western Germany only), NO_x emissions in 1990 amounted to 4.3 kg/US$ 1 000 (1985), versus an OECD average of 3.8. NO_x emissions per capita (for western Germany only) were also slightly above the OECD average at 46.7 kg/cap. versus 44.3.

Particulates

Particulates emissions arise primarily from the burning of coal and oil. Total particulates emissions in Germany fell from 2.9 million tons in 1980 to 2.2 million in 1990. Reduction of particulates is particularly susceptible to technological control. The secular shift in the fuel mix in the old Länder, along with the continued introduction of particulate pollution control devices, has contributed greatly to the one-third decline in national particulates pollution levels.

About 95 per cent (2.1 million tons) of total particulates emissions come from stationary sources, with mobile sources accounting for only 107 kt. This represents very little change in relative sectoral contributions since 1980, when stationary sources accounted for some 2.7 million tons of particulates and mobile sources only 99 kt. Some 85 per cent of total particulate emissions are in the new Länder, reflecting a greater use of brown coal, and less widespread, less sophisticated use of particulate emissions controls.

The reduction in emissions in the old Länder in the 1980s, though significant, has resulted in uneven reductions in concentrations of particulates (micrograms/m^3), as measured in selected western German cities. Using 1980 as an index base year, concentrations by 1989 had fallen from 100 to 98 in West Berlin, 68 in Frankfurt, and 81 in Gelsenkirchen.

D. JAPAN

ENERGY TAX PROFILE

Energy-related taxes in Japan are levied at both the national and local level. They comprise, at the national level, consumption taxes on specific fuels (gasoline, liquefied petroleum gas (LPG), aviation fuel, and petroleum), various taxes on motor vehicles, customs duties on oil, and a tax on sales of electricity to fund power plant construction and petroleum substitution. There is also a general consumption tax, which has special provisions for certain energy services. At the local level (municipalities and prefectures), energy-related taxes include primarily vehicle taxes, and a local road tax levied on gasoline sales; local governments also share in the receipts of various national taxes.

One hallmark of the Japanese energy tax system is that revenues from each excise tax are earmarked for a specific purpose: the gasoline tax and the LPG auto fuel tax, for road construction and maintenance; the aviation fuel tax, for airport construction and maintenance; the petroleum tax, for energy security including alternative resource and technology development, and most notably for building strategic oil reserves; the customs duty on oil, for coal industry support and reclamation work; and the electricity tax, for research on diversification of generating sources and for siting and safety measures related to nuclear power development.

Energy production tax incentives are generally administered through the income tax system. Such measures include special oil company tax depreciation allowances for anti-pollution facilities, oil desulfurisation facilities and for sophisticated production facilities such as cracking units, for which tax credits are also available. Special depreciation allowances are also available for investment in solar and energy saving equipment.

National taxes

Consumption-related taxes

General consumption tax

The general consumption tax, effective since 1989, is assessed at a rate of 3 per cent on consumption of goods and service. The tax is a simple flat rate with the exception of a 4.5 per cent rate on certain passenger vehicles.

Like the VAT applied in European countries, this tax is ultimately levied on households, commercial and industrial enterprises being eligible for VAT rebates or exemptions. The scheme thus avoids cumulative taxation through deduction of taxes on intermediate purchases. Special taxes, also deductible as business expenses by those eligible for VAT refunds, include the gasoline tax and the LPG tax. The light oil delivery tax is not levied on businesses, but only on household consumers.

Transactions are subject to the general consumption tax if they are domestic, constitute a business activity, are effected for compensation, and are categorized as the sales or leasing of assets or provision of services. In the case of services pertaining to research, planning, and aspects of management requiring specialized, professional knowledge in science and technology and made in connection with the construction or production of facilities for the transformation and distribution of electrical current, the storage and supply of gas, and the storage of oil, the determination of whether a transaction is domestic depends on where most of the materials needed for the construction or production of the facilities are procured.

Customs duties

A customs duty of 315 Yen/kl is levied on all imported crude oil and petroleum products. Established in 1980 to fund financial assistance to the coal industry, it is being phased out and is proposed to expire in 2001. In 1991 revenues from customs duties were estimated to be 110 billion Yen.

Energy consumption excise taxes

There are four major national taxes levied on petroleum products delivered within Japan: the gasoline/local road tax, an aviation fuel tax, a

tax on LPG, and the petroleum tax. Diesel fuel is taxed only at the prefectural level. There is also a tax levied on electricity. No tax is levied on
coal (except the 3 per cent consumption tax).

Total taxes on the various fuels and for different consumers reflect
different excise tax rates and different tax obligations under the VAT. All
petroleum products are subject to identical excise taxes levied on a per
unit volume (kl) basis: an import duty, the light fuel oil tax, and the
petroleum tax. On top of these, the 3 per cent consumption tax is levied,
which is an ad valorem tax, and so varies with final price, reflecting
among other things the difference between wholesale and retail prices
charged respectively to industry and to households.

Gasoline tax

The gasoline tax is imposed on fuel shipped from refineries or
withdrawn from bonded storage, at a tax rate of 45,600 Yen/kl. The ship-
per, or the one who withdraws the gasoline from bond is liable for the tax.

Gasoline used in a refinery or bonded area is taxed as though
shipped, but exemptions are provided for exports, and for shipments to
and from other refineries. Gasoline consumed as a raw material for petrochemicals or for electric power generation is not subject to this tax.

Roughly three-quarters of the revenue from the gasoline tax is collected into the General Account of the State and roughly one-quarter into
the Special Account for Road Construction and Improvement, earmarked
for road construction and maintenance. In 1991, revenues from the gasoline tax amounted to an estimated 2 trillion Yen.

Local road tax

The local road tax is a transfer tax levied nationally and allocated
to local governments for road improvement. It is paid and collected along
with the gasoline tax. The tax base is the same as for gasoline but the tax
rate is different: 8,200 Yen/kl. In 1991, revenues from the local road tax
amounted to some 366 billion Yen.

Aviation fuel tax

This tax is levied on fuel loaded into aircraft for domestic flights
including helicopters, but exempting national and local government use of

aircraft. The tax rate is 26,000 Yen/kl, payable by the owners, users, pilots-in-command, or persons who test or repair aircraft engines.

In 1991 revenues from this tax amounted to some 77 billion Yen. Of this, 65 billion Yen went to the General Account of the State and to the Airport Construction and Improvement Special Account, and some 12 billion Yen was distributed to local governments for the prevention of aircraft noise disturbance and for local airport improvements.

Liquefied petroleum tax

This tax is levied on the sales of LPG as fuel for automobiles, and is imposed at a rate of 17.5 Yen per kilogram (or per litre where sold by volume, one litre being considered as 0.56 kg). Methane and ethane are not subject to this tax.

The tax is paid by the retail distributor, with exemptions for exports and refunds for gas reshipped to a filling station, as with gasoline. In 1991, revenues from this tax amounted to an estimated 34 billion Yen, one half of which was, by law, distributed to local governments as a transfer tax earmarked for road expenditures.

Petroleum tax

The petroleum tax is levied on domestic oil and gas production, and on imports of crude oil, gaseous hydrocarbons and petroleum products (to avoid discrimination against products manufactured from crude oil subject to the tax). Petroleum products that are taxed include petroleum spirits, kerosenes, gas oils, heavy fuel oils and raw oils, lubricating oils, and greases.

The tax is paid by those who ship from domestic extracting stations or who withdraw imported commodities subject to the tax from bonded areas. However, there are a number of exceptions. Exports, and shipments of gaseous hydrocarbons by extractors for their own exclusive use, are not subject to the tax. Shipments of hydrocarbons between extracting stations, shipments of domestically produced naphtha as a raw material for petrochemicals, and domestically produced heavy fuel oil used in agriculture, forestry or fishery, are all eligible for refunds of the petroleum tax.

The tax is levied on the quantity of crude petroleum or gaseous hydrocarbons shipped from extracting stations or withdrawn from bonded areas. The tax rates are:

crude petroleum or imported petroleum products: 2,040 Yen/kl
natural gas: 720 Yen/t
gaseous hydrocarbons (except natural gas):   670 Yen/t

[Note: The rates cited here for natural gas and gaseous hydrocarbons are ultimately equivalent to those for petroleum, but are adjusted for a number of factors, including heat value.]

In 1991, revenues from the petroleum tax amounted to some 490 billion Yen. Estimated revenue figures for 1992 are 507 billion Yen. Revenues from the petroleum tax are collected into the General Account of the State, and transferred into the Petroleum and Alternative Energy Sources Account of the Special Account of Measures for Coal and Petroleum. In 1988, the petroleum tax was changed from an ad valorem to a per unit basis to stabilize the revenues for this fund.

Promotion of power-resource development tax

This tax is levied on the sales of electric power by ordinary electric utility enterprises, excepting sales or transfers to other ordinary utilities, and on volumes of electricity consumed by each ordinary utility (except for the generation of electric power). The tax rate is 445 Yen/1 000 KWh of electricity sold.

The tax is imposed according to the volume of electricity generated regardless of the source. Electricity from hydro, geothermal and nuclear power sources is thus taxed.

Revenues are used partly to fund construction of nuclear power plant sitings, safety and environmental programmes, and partly to fund electricity diversification measures including solar, geothermal and fuel cell research. In 1991, the revenues from this tax amounted to some 298 billion Yen.

Motor vehicle taxes

Although these do not constitute energy taxes *per se*, they are energy-related inasmuch as rates are roughly related to the fuel consuming characteristics of the vehicles.

A motor vehicle tonnage tax is imposed on any vehicle for which an inspection certificate or a registration number is required, and is collected at the time of inspection or registration. Tax rates vary according to type of vehicle, use, size and cylinder capacity, and range from a low of 1,700 Yen for a motorcycle used for business, to a high of 18,900 Yen for each half ton of vehicle weight for a private passenger-carrying vehicle other than a light motor vehicle. Large special-type vehicles such as bull-dozers, and used light motor vehicles requiring no inspection are exempt from the tax.

The motor vehicle tonnage tax is collected into the General Account of the State, and is shared with local governments. Twenty-five percent of receipts are earmarked for local use in the construction and improvement of local roads. In 1991, some 853 billion Yen were collected from this tax, of which about 213 billion Yen were given to local government.

Production-related taxes

Most energy producer taxes and tax concessions are tied to the corporate income tax scheme. Main exceptions to this are direct subsidies to coal and to nuclear power, earmarked from revenues from the petroleum tax, custom duties and the tax on electricity.

Energy producer income tax provisions

Along with some other industries, energy producers are permitted tax deferral on certain reserves deductible as expenses. These include reserves for losses of overseas investment in natural resource development, for electric utilities for removal and disposal of nuclear facilities, for gas utilities for construction of specified gas distribution facilities, for companies involved in the reprocessing of nuclear fuel, for hydroelectric companies against losses due to drought, and for the closing down of oil and gas fields at sea, including removal of rigs and prevention of pollution. It should be noted, however, that while these items are specific to the energy industry, they do not necessarily constitute undue preferences; they generally reflect business expenses to the various energy producers.

There are also special depreciation provisions available for investment in solar power and in energy conservation and related equipment. These permit initial depreciation of 30 per cent of acquisition cost in addition to ordinary depreciation. In 1991 tax expenditures under this provision were an estimated 84 billion Yen.

Investment tax credit

An investment tax credit is available to businesses for the purchase of equipment needed to respond to changes in energy circumstances. The tax credit is 7 per cent of the equipment acquisition cost, limited to a maximum of 20 per cent of total corporate tax liability in a given year.

Subsidies

Japan, like several other coal producing countries, provides direct and indirect subsidies to its domestic coal producers, some of which constitutes direct aid to current production, and some of which is aimed at facilitating a rationalisation of the industry, with attendant aid for worker retraining and economic development in mining areas affected by structural adjustment.

Aid to current production is given in the form of grants for modernising coal pits, for stabilising the coal industry, for improving safety conditions and for paying off interest on loans. Such aid amounted to some 16.7 billion Yen for fiscal year 1990/91, and is expected to be about 15.2 billion Yen for fiscal year 1991/92.

Effective price supports on coal consumed by electricity producers, non-ferrous industries, iron and steel producers, and by coke and gas coke producers, amounted to some 108.9 billion Yen in fiscal year 1990/91, and is estimated at 103.1 billion Yen for fiscal year 1991/92.

These two subsidy programs together constitute the total Producer Subsidy Equivalent (PSE) used by the OECD to calculate the distorting effects of production-related subsidies. The total PSE for Japanese coal thus amounted to 125.6 billion and 118.3 billion Yen for the fiscal years 1990/91 and 1991/92 respectively.

This amounts to 15,739 Yen per ton of coal produced and 12,230 Yen per ton of coal sold in 1990/91. Comparable figures for 1991/92 are estimated to be 14,427 Yen and 12,720 Yen respectively.

Total assistance to the coal industry, including aid other than to direct production, amounted to some 213 billion Yen in fiscal year 1990/91, and 200 billion Yen in fiscal year 1991/92.

Local taxes

Consumption related taxes

Prefectural light-oil delivery tax

This tax is levied on deliveries of diesel fuel or light-oil from a refiner, importer, or from certain wholesalers. It is collected by the seller at the time of delivery, along with the charge for the oil; the present tax rate is 24,300 Yen/kl of light-oil.

All diesel fuel including automotive diesel is subject to this tax, with a few exceptions, primarily for off-road uses of automotive diesel. These include fuel for ships, railway engines and for agricultural and forestry machinery, and exports. The revenues are earmarked to fund local road projects and are shared with cities. In 1991, these revenues amounted to an estimated 860 billion Yen.

Prefectural automobile acquisition tax

This is one of several asset acquisition taxes collected at the pre-fectural level. It is levied on the purchase price (or imputed value in the case of a gift) of every automobile sale (except acquisition of automobiles by national or local government entities, and except for certain special or two-wheeled automobiles). The rate is 3 per cent of the purchase price in most cases, and 5 per cent for certain non-commercial motor vehicles. Vehicles costing less than 500,000 Yen are exempt.

Revenues are shared by the prefectures and municipal govern-ments, and are earmarked for their respective road expenditures. The municipal share will range from 70-95 per cent. In fiscal year 1991 reve-nues from this tax were 575 billion Yen; revenues in fiscal year 1992 amounted to some 620 billion Yen.

Prefectural automobile tax

This annual tax is levied on each person in a prefecture owning an automobile. The tax rate varies according to the type of vehicle, use and cylinder capacity, and ranges from 4,500 Yen for three-wheeled cars used for commercial purposes, to 111,000 Yen for cars with a cylinder volume over 6,000 cc used for non-commercial purposes. In 1991 revenues from this tax amounted to some 1.3 trillion Yen.

Municipal light vehicle tax

This tax is levied on motorbikes, motorcycles and light two-, three- and four-wheeled vehicles, at rates ranging from 1,000 Yen for motorbikes to 7,200 Yen for four-wheeled passenger cars used for non-commercial purposes. Revenues from these taxes in 1991 amounted to some 91 billion Yen.

Summary of revenues

The revenues from the various excise taxes on energy in fiscal year 1991 amounted to some 3.4 trillion Yen at the national level and 860 billion Yen at the Prefectural and local level. National taxes on energy accounted for some 5.2 per cent of total national revenues (65 trillion Yen). Local taxes on energy accounted for less than one per cent of locally collected tax revenues.

Motor vehicle taxes were another 2.3 trillion Yen, over 60 per cent (almost 2 trillion Yen) of which was collected in Prefectural taxes. These taxes at the national level comprise just over 1 per cent of total national revenues. Motor vehicle taxes are more important at the Prefectural level, comprising over 4 per cent of locally collected tax revenues.

ENERGY PROFILE[1]

Japan is the world's largest importer of coal and liquefied natural gas. As of 1990, net imports provided about 85 per cent of Japan's total primary energy supply. Domestic fossil fuel production accounted for 1.6 per cent of TPES.

The changes in Japan's TPES from 1979 to 1990 are shown in Figure 1. Figure 2 shows relative fuel shares in TPES in 1990. Most notable of the changes taking place in the energy mix in the intervening decade are a dramatic drop in the share of oil, and a doubling in the shares of gas and of nuclear power generation. By 1990 nuclear generation of electricity accounted for 12 per cent of TPES.

Figure 1: **Total TPES and TPES by fuel in Japan, 1979 and 1990**

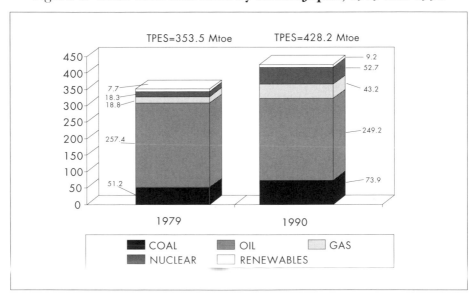

1 - The figures in this section are taken from IEA statistics *Energy Policies of IEA Countries, 1991 Review*, and do not necessarily conform to national statistics by virtue of differences in definitions, estimation and/or measurement. IEA figures have been used in the case studies whenever possible, for purposes of comparibility.

Figure 2: **Fuel Shares in TPES in Japan, 1990**

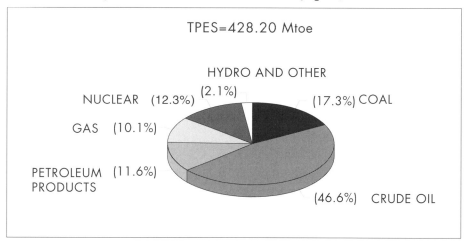

TPES=428.20 Mtoe

HYDRO AND OTHER
(2.1%)
NUCLEAR (12.3%)
(17.3%) COAL
GAS (10.1%)
PETROLEUM (11.6%)
PRODUCTS
(46.6%) CRUDE OIL

By contrast, net imports in 1979 accounted for 90 per cent of TPES. In that year nuclear generation of electricity accounted for 5 per cent of TPES.

Electricity generation increased 46 per cent from 1979 to 1990. Notable changes in the generating mix during that time are a drop in oil-fired generation, a doubling of nuclear generation and almost a doubling of coal-fired generation. Figure 3 shows the generating mix for Japanese utilities for 1990.

Figure 3: **Fuel shares in electricity output in Japan, 1990**

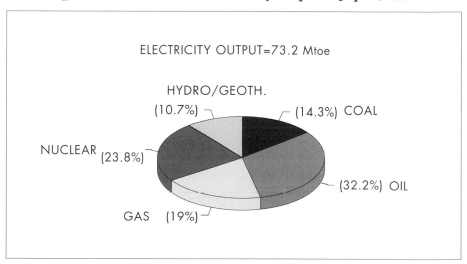

ELECTRICITY OUTPUT=73.2 Mtoe

HYDRO/GEOTH.
(10.7%)
(14.3%) COAL
NUCLEAR
(23.8%)
(32.2%) OIL
GAS (19%)

Note that by 1990, coal accounted for about 14 per cent of the generating mix in Japan, despite a decline in production. The government intends to foster coal-fired generation as its second most important (after nuclear) base load supply source.

Natural gas-fired generation increased some 50 percent from 1979 to 1990, reflecting a continued effort to reduce oil dependence, and growing environmental concerns. The generating sector now accounts for some 66 per cent of gas consumption in Japan. An even greater share of gas-fired generation is planned, largely for environmental reasons. Except for hydro-power, renewables at present are a negligible part of the generating mix and of TPES.

Figure 4 shows the changes in energy consumption between 1979 and 1990. Figure 5 shows the fuel mix for final consumption in 1990. The drop in oil consumption reflects Japan's concerted efforts, like those of other OECD countries, to reduce the share of oil in the energy mix. Oil's share has declined in the past decade in virtually every sector except transport. Sectoral shares in final consumption are shown in Figure 6.

Figure 4: **Total TFC and TFC by fuel in Japan, 1979 and 1990**

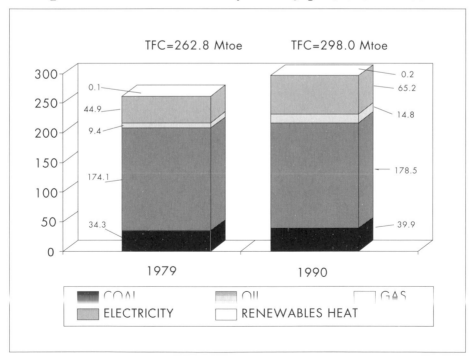

Figure 5: **Fuel Shares in TFC in Japan, 1990**

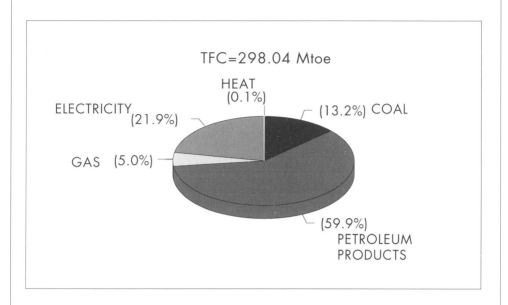

TFC=298.04 Mtoe

HEAT (0.1%)

ELECTRICITY (21.9%)

(13.2%) COAL

GAS (5.0%)

(59.9%) PETROLEUM PRODUCTS

Figure 6: **TFC by sector in Japan, 1990**

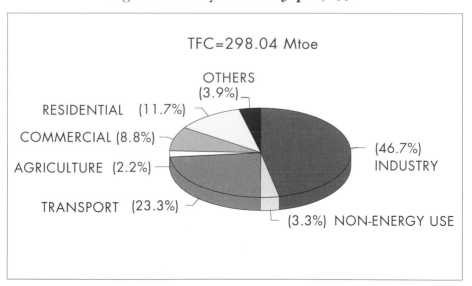

TFC=298.04 Mtoe

OTHERS (3.9%)

RESIDENTIAL (11.7%)

COMMERCIAL (8.8%)

AGRICULTURE (2.2%)

(46.7%) INDUSTRY

TRANSPORT (23.3%)

(3.3%) NON-ENERGY USE

ENERGY-RELATED POLLUTION PROFILE[2]

Statistics on most energy-related pollution in Japan are only available for 1980-86, and do not reflect more recent improvements in pollution control. Nevertheless, the statistics available for the pollutants of interest here - CO_2, SO_2, NO_x and particulates - indicate that volumes of energy-related pollution in Japan have been falling except for CO_2. The rise in CO_2 emissions reflects in part the steady growth in Japanese energy consumption throughout the decade 1980-1990.

CO_2 emissions

Energy-related emissions of CO_2 in Japan were higher in 1990 than in 1980 (1.1 billion tons of CO_2 vs. 940 million), reflecting a general rise in energy consumption resulting from a boom in the Japanese economy and from lower oil prices. The share of stationary source emissions remained virtually unchanged over the decade at 79 per cent of total emissions.

The only major drop in stationary source emissions came in the industrial sector, where emissions dropped by 100 million tons, from 278 million to 179 million in ten years. Emissions from the transformation sector, however, grew almost 25 per cent, from 283 million tons to 351 million.

CO_2 emissions from mobile sources in 1980 amounted to 193 million tons, some 20 per cent of total emissions in that year. By 1990, mobile source emissions had risen to 217 million tons, but still accounted for some 20 per cent of total CO_2 emissions in Japan.

2 - The statistics for CO_2 used in these Energy-Related Pollution Profiles have been compiled and calculated by the IEA/OECD as current but as yet unpublished updates of the statistics in the *OECD Environmental Data Compendium 1991*, and may not correspond exactly with national statistics. The statistics on other pollutants in Japan are taken from the *Compendium* and may not correspond with national statistics.

The ratio of CO_2 emissions to GDP in Japan in 1988 was 181 kg/US\$ 1 000 (1985), well below the OECD average of 286 kg/US\$ 1 000 (1985). The ratio of CO_2 emissions per capita for Japan in 1988 was 2.2 kg/cap., also well below the OECD average of 3.4.

SO_2 emissions

Sulfur dioxide emissions in Japan fell from 1263 kt in 1980 to 835 kt in l986. SO_2 emissions from mobile sources actually rose in this timeframe (from 119 kt to 151 kt), but gains in the stationary source sector can be considered dramatic. Stationary source emissions fell from 1144 kt in 1980 to 684 kt in 1986, a drop of 40 per cent. By 1986, stationary sources still accounted for 82 per cent of all SO_2 emissions, but less than the 91 per cent of 1980. These gains can be attributed in part to pollution control throughout the decade, including fuel mix changes. In fiscal year 1992, for example, some 191 billion Yen will be spent for oil substitution in electricity generation.

Emissions of SO_2 per unit of GDP in Japan by 1989 were 0.6 kg/US\$ 1 000 (1985) vs. the OECD average of 4.1. SO_2 emissions per capita in Japan by 1989 were 6.8/kg/cap. vs. the OECD average of 48.3.

Progress in emissions control for SO_2 is clearly reflected in the indexed changes in SO_2 concentrations measured in various Japanese cities. Using a base year of 1980=100, by 1988, SO_2 concentrations (micrograms/m^3) in Tokyo had fallen to 40, in Kawasaki to 68, in Kanazawa to 65, with the national average having fallen to 50.

NO_x emissions

As for nitrogen oxide pollution, total emissions in Japan fell from 1400 kt in 1980 to 1176 kt in 1986, reflecting gains in both mobile and stationary sources. NO_x from mobile sources fell from 601 kt in 1980 to 514 kt in 1986, while stationary source emissions in that same period fell from 799 kt to 662 kt. The relative contributions of the two sectors to total emissions have not changed, with stationary sources accounting for some 46-47 per cent of emissions and mobile sources 53-54 per cent.

Emissions of NO_x per unit of GDP in Japan were 0.8 kg/US\$ 1 000 (1985) by 1989; per capita emissions by 1989 were 9.6 kg/cap. OECD averages for these same ratios by 1989 were 3.8 kg/US\$ 1 000 (1985) and 44.3 kg/cap.

Progress in controlling the effects of these NO_x emissions on a geographic basis, however, has been more spotty than indicated by these sectoral emissions gains. The indexed measures of NO_x concentrations (micrograms/m³) in selected Japanese cities do not yet reflect the reductions in emissions noted above. With 1980 as the base year (1980 = 100), concentrations of NO_x by 1988 were 97 in Tokyo, after having fallen to 86 in 1985; and were 93 in Kanazawa, also after having fallen to a low of 85 in 1986. In Kawasaki, concentrations by 1988 had reached an index level of 124, having fallen to 94 in 1982. The national average for NO_x concentrations by 1988 was 102, again with a decline through 1985, followed by a rise to record high levels in 1987 and 1988. These trends reflect both a growth in urbanization and strong economic growth.

Particulates

Statistics on emissions of particulates in Japan were not available to this study, however, available data on concentrations indicate very little reduction. With 1982 = 100 as an index base year, the national average of particulates concentrations (micrograms/m³) in 1988 was still 100, and concentrations in Kawasaki were 98. With 1980 = 100 as the base year, concentration levels in Tokyo had reached 110 by 1988, and those in Kanazawa 104.

These end-of-period figures, however, mask large variations in local concentrations over time, with levels in Tokyo, for example, having reached a low in 1983 of 98 and a high in 1987 of 123. Variations in concentrations in Kanazawa are also notable, with levels having fallen steadily to a low of 80 in 1985, then rising to a high of 108 in 1987. Kawasaki shows similar fluctuations, with a low of 88 in 1985 and a high of 106 in 1987. The national average fluctuates somewhat less, rising and falling throughout the period between concentration index values of 94 and 104 micrograms/m³.

E. THE UNITED STATES

ENERGY TAX PROFILE

The US has no VAT or general consumption tax. Taxes on energy use in the United States consist primarily of excise taxes on fuels for transport, some levied by the Federal government and some by the States.

As of 1991, there are energy-related Federal excise taxes on motor vehicle, rail, and aviation fuels, recreational and commercial boat fuels, and on gasoline for non-commercial outdoor power equipment. Taxes are also levied on crude oil and hazardous chemicals for the Superfund clean up of waste sites, for leaking underground storage tanks and for the oil spill liability fund. Finally, there is a tax on coal to fund black lung compensation. Motor vehicle taxes are levied at the Federal level on gas guzzling cars.

State and local governments levy energy taxes including excise taxes on motor fuels, sales taxes on coal, natural gas deliveries and electricity, and state severance taxes. They also levy taxes on motor vehicles, including registration and license fees.

A number of energy-related tax credits, subsidies and tax exemptions also exist, primarily for energy production and production-related investment. There is an investment tax credit (accelerated depreciation and expenditure deductions) for enhanced oil and gas recovery and for solar and geothermal energy producing properties; oil and gas depletion and intangible drilling cost allowances; and alternative fuel production credits covering oil and gas produced from non-conventional sources, especially methane from coal seams. There are tax credits for commuting and energy conservation, subsidies for rural electrification and public power, low-income home-energy assistance, and subsidies for research into clean coal technology.

Federal taxes

Consumption related taxes

Energy consumption excises

Taxes on Motor fuels

The Federal tax code governing energy-related excise taxes and tax concessions was revised as of 1 January 1991, as part of the Omnibus Budget Reconciliation Act of 1990. At the same time, some excise taxes were increased as part of a deficit reduction scheme. The following table shows these changes in excise taxes on motor fuels; note that these are rates per gallon regardless of the base price of the fuel.

US motor fuel excise taxes 1990-91
(cents/gallon)

Specified Fuel	1990	1991	% Change
Motor gasoline (except for off-the road/farm use)	9	14	+56
Motor diesel	15	20	+33
Special motor fuels (benzol, benzene. naphtha, LPG, casinghead and natural gas)	9	14	+568
Methanol fuels from other than petroleum or natural gas	3	8	+1678
Ethanol from other than petroleum or natural gas	3	8.6	+187
Fuels from natural gas	4.5	7	+56
Gasohol from ethanol	3.33	9.56	+18
Gasohol from other than ethanol	3.33	8.99	+170
Diesel oil	9	14.6	+62
Diesel rail fuel	0	2.50	

Source: Schedule of Present Federal Excise Taxes (as of January, 1, 1991) - Government
Committee on Taxation. March 1. 1991

Of the increases, 2.5¢/gallon is allocated to deficit reduction for a 5-year period, after which time that portion of the levy expires. The remainder of the monies are virtually all allocated to the Highway Trust Fund and its several sub-funds, including 1.5¢ per gallon to the mass transit fund. Revenues generated by motor gasoline and diesel taxes amounted to some US$ 15 billion in 1991 for the Highway Trust Fund and US$ 2.4 billion for the General Fund (deficit reduction). Estimates for 1992 are US$ 15.5 billion and US$ 3.2 billion respectively.

Motor fuels taxes are essentially collected from wholesalers with the cost of recouping the tax being deductible as a business expense against Federal and some State income taxes. Federal gasoline taxes have traditionally been collected at bulk terminals, called rack points, which handle bulk transfers either by pipeline or marine vessel, and at which points measurement "breaks bulk", i.e. goes from barrels (wholesale) to gallons (retail).

Only diesel used for motor fuel is subject to excise taxes, and off-road motor diesel use is eligible for a tax refund. Diesel used for home heating is not excisable.

Evasion of motor fuel excise taxes in the US is considered a serious problem. The Department of Transportation estimates annual collection shortfalls ranging from 3-7 per cent for gasoline and 12-20 per cent for diesel fuel. The higher rate of tax evasion for diesel fuel reflects both motive (higher tax rates make non-payment more profitable) and opportunity (the number of exempted uses makes non-payment more feasible).

As shown in the preceding and following tables, alcohol-based fuels enjoy a partial exemption from the excise taxes on highway motor fuels, and on aviation fuel; they also have partial exemptions for payments to the LUST[1] Fund. These preferences were created to encourage manufacture and use of alternative motor fuels, and have been retained even though all fuel excise taxes have been raised.

Taxes on alcohol-based motor fuels are collected on wholesale sales like diesel motor fuel taxes. Composition must be certificated to qualify for differentiated excise tax rates.

Aviation fuels taxes

Excise taxes on aviation fuels for non-commercial aviation have been increased along with those of motor fuels, as shown in the table

---

1 Leaking Underground Storage Tank Trust Fund.

below. Taxes on commercial aviation are levied as a percentage of passenger ticket prices and/or of air cargo rates.

Increases in excise on aviation fuel - 1990-1991
(cents/gallon)

Specified Fuel	1990	1991
Gasoline	12	15
Non-gasoline (jet fuel)	14	17.8
Non-gasoline (alcohol/ethanol methane)	0	4.56
Non-gasoline (alcohol/non-ethanol methane)	0	3.89

Aviation fuel excise taxes are collected on wholesale sales at different rates according to use. These excise taxes are allocated primarily into the Airport and Airway Trust Fund, except that 2.5¢/gallon will be allocated to the General Fund for deficit reduction until 1995. In 1991, revenues were US$ 130 million for the Trust Fund and US$ 26 million for deficit reduction; for 1992, estimates are US$ 124 million and US$ 32 million respectively.

Boat and miscellaneous fuel taxes

Gasoline and special fuels used in motorboats and in small-engine outdoor power tools (for non-business use) are also subject to motor fuels excises. All revenues from motorboats are dedicated to the Aquatic Resources Trust Fund. Revenues from the tax on gasoline for power tools go to the Sport Fish Restoration Account of the Highway Trust Fund, to be available for the wetlands environmental program. In 1991, the Aquatic Trust Fund excise taxes from motorboat fuel were an estimated US$ 138 million, expected to rise to US$ 151 million in 1992. Taxes on gasoline used in small engines is expected to raise US$ 41 million in 1991 for the Trust Fund, and US$ 50 million in 1992.

The excise taxes on diesel and other liquid fuels used by commercial cargo vessels on specified waterways will progressively be raised from

13 cents per gallon in 1991 to 20 cents per gallon by 1995. Revenues are dedicated to the Inland Waterways Trust Fund. In 1990, these revenues amounted to US$ 63 million, some US$ 60 million in 1991, and an estimated US$ 70 million in 1992.

Oil spill and clean-up taxes

Three separate excise taxes are levied on crude oil and oil products to cover damages from various kinds of petroleum spills: Superfund excise taxes, LUST Fund taxes and Oil Spill Liability Trust Fund excises.

Superfund excise taxes of 9.7 cents per barrel of domestic or imported crude oil or petroleum products are in effect until 1995. These taxes constitute oil's contribution to the Superfund, a national programme to clean up hazardous waste dumps resulting from poor chemical management in the past. Similar contributions are levied on all corporations paying the alternative minimum tax: they are not just collected from energy producers or products.

Excise taxes are also collected on oil products through the Leaking Underground Storage Tank Trust Fund (known as LUST funds), to provide relief from damages due to widespread leaking of chemical and petroleum storage tanks into soil and ground and surface waters. The LUST Fund was enacted as part of the Superfund Revenue Act of 1986.

LUST Fund tax rates are 0.1 cent per gallon for all ordinary motor gasoline (but excluding LPG), and a tax of 0.05 cent per gallon on methanol and ethanol fuels (with a content of at least 85 per cent methanol or ethanol). Lower rates were deliberately established for alcohol fuels as an incentive to their production and use. In 1991, revenues to the LUST Fund were US$ 123 million; the estimate for 1992 is US$ 145 million.

The excise tax for the Oil Spill Liability Trust Fund, in effect since January 1990, is levied on domestic or imported crude oil and imported petroleum products at a rate of 5¢ per barrel. Revenues to the Fund in 1991 were some US$ 254 million, with US$ 283 million estimated for 1992.

Superfund taxes are collected on domestic crude oil when it is received at the refinery and on imported crude oil and products at customs at the point of entry. Taxes for the Oil Spill Liability Fund are collected as an add-on rate to the Superfund tax. LUST fund taxes on gasoline, diesel and alcohol fuels are collected as an add-on to the relevant highway, rail and aviation fuel excise taxes.

Coal excise taxes

An excise tax is levied on hard coal but not on lignite or brown coal from U.S. mines, to provide for the Black Lung Disability Trust Fund, to fund compensation to health-impaired coal miners. Like the Superfund, this tax was designed to clean up a legacy of past damages. The current tax is US$ 1.10 per ton on coal from underground mines and US$ 0.55 per ton on coal from surface mines, with a ceiling on the tax equivalent to 4.4 per cent of the price of the coal as sold by the producer. Current rates include surcharges imposed in 1985 to restore the solvency of the Fund. Once the fund is solvent or after 1 January 2014 (whichever is earlier), rates revert to their original pre-1982 levels of US$ 0.50/ton for underground mines and US$ 0.25/ton for surface mines, and a cap on the rates equivalent to 2 per cent of the current producer's price. In 1991, these taxes amounted to US$ 652 million; the estimate for 1992 is US$ 627 million.

There is also a 2 cent/ton fee levied on coal to fund the Abandoned Mine Reclamation Fund, available to correct past environmental damages to ground and ground waters caused by coal extraction.

Gas guzzler tax

The US has not traditionally levied motor vehicle taxes at the national level. The Federal government does, however, impose an excise tax on cars which do not meet statutory standards for fuel economy, called "gas guzzlers". This tax puts a price on greater than average fuel consumption, which is deemed socially undesirable, and is intended to effect some internalisation of fuel-related pollution costs. It has nothing to do with the standards set for car manufacturers known as CAFE standards, which prescribe average fleet efficiency. Instead, it is levied on individual vehicles of any model with greater than average fuel consumption. It encourages consumers to purchase fuel-efficient vehicles.

The gas guzzler tax was doubled under the 1990 Act, raising the tax to US$ 1 000 per vehicle for those with a fuel economy rating between 21.5-22.5 miles per gallon (mpg), with increases in the tax rate to a maximum of US$ 7 700 per vehicle for those with a rating of less than 12.5 mpg. The tax is imposed on the manufacturer or importer and generally applies to passenger automobiles with unloaded gross weights of

6 000 pounds or less. The 1990 Act specifically made all limousines, including previously exempt stretch limousines, subject to the tax regardless of their weight. In 1991 this excise tax raised some estimated US$ 102 million in revenues; it is expected to increase to US$ 115 million in 1992.

Production-related taxes

All corporations, including energy producers, are subject to federal corporate income tax at the rate of 34 per cent with allowances and adjustments for legitimate business expenses, and with some tax preferences for energy production, as listed below. Most of these tax preferences take the form of accelerated depreciation, and some are analogous to allowances granted for other industries.

Subsidies

Tax preference for extractive industries - oil, gas, coal.

Under normal rules for cost recovery, capital assets cannot be fully deducted when purchased but are written off at a prescribed rate over the anticipated useful life of the asset either as depletion or depreciation. Oil and gas wells and mineral mines enjoy two principal special rules for cost recovery: the expensing of certain exploration and development costs, and percentage depletion.

Rules for expensing costs permit the immediate write-off of costs for excavating mines and for drilling wells, including what are called intangible drilling costs, rather than requiring their capitalization and slower write-off through depreciation. Independent oil and gas producers and non-corporate producers can expense all of their exploration and development costs. For integrated oil and gas companies, expensing is limited to 75 per cent of eligible costs, with the remaining 25 per cent subject to depletion over a five year period.

Under percentage depletion, eligible independent and non-corporate producers are permitted to deduct annually a certain percentage of a property's gross income regardless of actual capitalised costs. The deduction is now limited to 15 per cent of the gross income from the first 1 000 barrels per day of oil and gas production. Write-offs can exceed capitalised costs. The rationale given for this allowance is that independents are likely to be the ones producing from marginal properties, where continued exploration is deemed desirable.

Coal and uranium producers are also eligible for percentage depletion. They may deduct 10 per cent on new ventures, with this allowance limited to 50 per cent of the net income from the mineral property after production costs.

It is estimated that the expensing of exploration and development could cost the Treasury some US$ 50 million in foregone revenue in 1992, and some US$ 100 billion in 1993. Percentage depletion as now permitted is estimated to have cost some US$ 100 million in lost revenue in 1992, and is expected to cost the same in 1993.

Enhanced oil recovery credit

This investment tax credit is designed to encourage tertiary recovery methods for oil production. It permits income tax deduction as current year expenses, of the cost of certain chemical injectants used to enhance the process of oil recovery, rather than their being capitalised and recovered through depreciation. This provision amounted to less than US$ 50 million in tax preferences in 1992 and is expected to stay at about that level.

Alternative fuel production credit

In order to encourage production of oil, gas and synthetic fuels from unconventional sources (tight sands, tar sands, coal seams, biomass, shale), a non-refundable credit of about US$ 4.75 is granted per barrel of oil equivalent production. The credit applies to the sources of the fuel rather than to the production method (in contrast to the enhanced oil recovery credit). It applies particularly to the drilling of the wells, material costs being covered by expensing. Gas production from coal seams is currently the largest beneficiary of this credit.

The available credit is tied to the price of oil with full credit available when the average price of oil is below US$ 23.50 (1979 dollars), phasing out to no credit when the wellhead price (in 1979 dollars) reaches US$ 29.50. This credit amounted to US$ 300 million in 1992, and is estimated to rise perhaps to some US$ 400 million in 1992.

Tax preferences for alcohol fuels

As noted above, alcohol fuels enjoy reduced rates for motor fuel excise taxes and for LUST Fund contributions. The sum cost to the Treasury of various alcohol fuel credits in 1992 amounted to some US$ 500 million, including US$ 400 million in reduction of excise tax receipts.

Energy investment credit for solar and geothermal property

Extended annually, this provision permits a non-refundable 10 per cent tax credit to businesses on investment in solar or geothermal energy property. The credit accrues to the business, not for being a generator of power, but for having chosen a non-fossil alternative for electricity generation.

Personal energy tax credits

Commuting expenses

Under present law, reimbursements for public transit costs provided by employers need not be counted as taxable income so long as the total value of the benefit does not exceed US$ 21 per month; if the benefit exceeds this ceiling, the exclusion is disallowed entirely and the entire value of the benefit is taxable as gross income. The entire value of employer-provided parking, in contrast, may be excluded from the employee's gross taxable income as a fringe benefit.

Residential energy conservation

Rate reductions given by utilities to customers participating in demand management programmes, and rebates given by utilities, manufacturers or retailers on the purchase of goods and services relating to energy conservation, may be excluded from gross income so long as the rebate is given directly to the buyer from the seller and not through or involving a third party. The residential energy tax credit has also been constrained so that only the portion of an expenditure on energy conservation or renewable energy source property not financed by subsidised energy financing or by any non-taxable government grants is eligible. Taxes losses related to these provisions are estimated to be negligible (less than US$ 50 million in 1992).

Rural Electrification Administration (REA)

Subsidies for rural electrification, in effect for some sixty years, are the only major energy-related subsidies not tied to the tax system. These comprise direct funding subsidies, low interest loans, federal loan insurance and federal loan guarantees, for loans averaging some US$ 1 billion per year. Treasury outlays to cover REA expenses in excess of repayment receipts have amounted to some US$ 200 million per year in recent years.

Royalties

The U. S. government collects royalty payments, rents and bonuses from the development and production of oil and gas on the Outer Continental Shelf (OCS), within U. S. territorial waters and beyond the jurisdiction of the states. In 1991, revenues from royalties amounted to some US$ 2.7 billion; from rents and bonuses, US$ 439 million. Unlike Australia and Denmark, the U.S. does not currently use taxes as an alternative to royalties to capture its share of the resource rents from OCS oil and gas production.

State Taxes

Consumption-related taxes

Since 1929, all states and many local governments in the U.S. levy excise taxes on motor fuels that parallel Federal taxes, but are generally higher. State motor fuel excise tax revenues have grown steadily, reflecting rising tax rates, but fluctuating with changes in demand for gasoline due to variations in oil prices and changes in car efficiency.

In 1992 state excise taxes for highway motor fuels ranged from 7.5 - 26 cents/gallon for gasoline; when sales and other state taxes are added, the state tax burden ranges from 8 - 29.9 cents/gallon. The average state excise tax is 17.8 cents/gallon and the weighted average is 16.9 cents/gallon. Average total state tax burden on motor fuels is 19 cents/gallon and the weighted average is 19.8 cents/gallon.

Many different exemptions are provided from state excise taxes on motor fuels: for fuel consumed for Federal government and sometimes for state or other government use, for charitable purposes and for public services, etc. As with Federal motor fuel excise taxes, exemptions are generally provided for non-motor fuel use and for off-highway (including agricultural) use, though the need to prevent tax avoidance often results in a refund or partial refund system rather than a direct exemption for non-highway gasoline use.

Virtually all state excise taxes collected on motor fuels are used to fund state highway maintenance programs and the improvement of local roads and streets. Even so, revenues from state and Federally-shared excise taxes amount to less than half of the total disbursement for these programs, the rest coming from general funds, toll roads, property taxes (including vehicle taxes in some states), local levies, income taxes, fees and bond issue proceeds secured by other than motor fuel taxes.

In addition to traditional specific excise taxes, several states impose sales taxes on certain energy products including motor fuels. Most states have their own LUST Fund tax with some that cover above-ground as well as underground storage, and a few notable states (California, Louisiana and Texas) have oil spill liability taxes levied as direct taxes on oil products. Most state excise taxes are fixed rate, per unit excise taxes, whereby revenues vary with volume but not with changing prices.

State revenues from motor fuels excise taxes were an estimated US$ 21 billion in 1991, with some US$ 22.6 billion expected in 1992. Total state revenues from motor fuel taxes including sales taxes, LUST Fund taxes etc, were an estimated US$ 24.6 billion in 1991; expected 1992 revenues are an estimated US$ 26.4 billion.

State sales taxes may also be levied on sales of electricity and natural gas at rates ranging from 2-6 per cent. Certain sales of light fuel oil and LPG for households are also taxed by some state and local governments. Total revenue figures for these taxes were not available for this study.

State severance and production-related taxes

Most producing states levy taxes on mineral fuel production known as severance taxes, production taxes, or privilege taxes, at an average rate of 6 per cent of the value of production. Producers of fuels and energy are also subject to standard state corporate property taxes, the latter being a major consideration in states which tax *in situ* reserves.

Percentage severance/production tax rates for oil and gas range from 0.04 per cent to 15 per cent of the value of the oil and gas produced; flat fee rates range from 0.001 to 15.2 cents per MCF of natural gas and from 0.005 to 80 cents per barrel of oil. For coal the rates also vary. In 1990, oil and gas tax collections amounted to some 85 per cent of total state resource production taxes. This amount has been climbing almost steadily over the years, reflecting at times both an increase in value of output and a periodic increase in the various tax rates.

ENERGY PROFILE[2]

The United States is a major energy producer and an even more significant consumer, largely (86 per cent) self-sufficient in total primary energy supply (TPES). The only major fuel in which the United States is not largely self-sufficient is crude oil, with domestic production in 1990 (425 Mtoe) accounting for only 56 per cent of total U. S. oil supply. Domestic production of natural gas by comparison, accounted for 95 per cent of 1990 gas supply. The United States is a net coal exporter, with 1990 net exports of 65 Mtoe amounting to 12 per cent of domestic production.

Figure 1: **Total TPES and TPES by fuel in the US, 1979 and 1990**

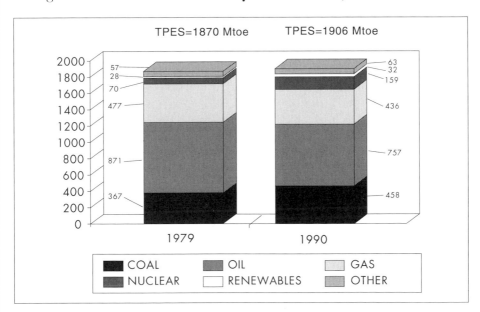

2 The figures in this section are taken from IEA statistics *Energy Policies of IEA Countries, 1991 Review,* and do not necessarily conform to national statistics by virtue of differences in definitions, estimation and/or measurement. IEA figures have been used in the case studies whenever possible, for purposes of comparability.

Figure 1 shows the changes in U. S. energy supply from 1979 to 1990, and Figure 2 shows the composition of TPES in 1990.

Figure 2: **Fuel Shares in TPES in the US, 1990**

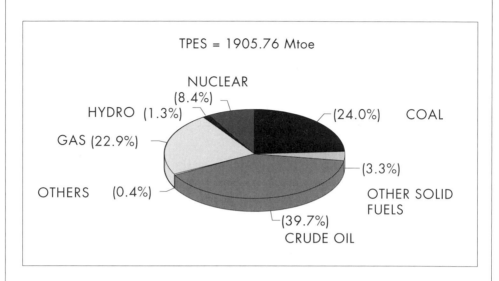

Non-fossil energy (nuclear, hydro, geothermal, solar) and non-coal solid fuels (wood and biomass) account for some 255 Mtoe or 13 per cent of TPES. Of these, wood and biomass are used primarily by industry and in residences. At 3 per cent of TPES, these represent a large share of total energy supply relative to other OECD countries. Nuclear, hydro, geothermal and solar (10 per cent of TPES) are used primarily for electricity generation.

Figure 3 shows the fuel mix for 1990 for electricity generation. Coal is the dominant fuel, followed by nuclear. Coal-fired generation has generally grown since 1985, for a variety of reasons. Perhaps most importantly, there was a concerted national policy to encourage the use of more coal and to use less oil to decrease U.S. dependence on oil imports. Other contributing factors included increases in efficiency of coal-fired generation, changes in natural gas regulation and absolute and relative fuel price changes. This increase in coal-fired generation also occurred despite increasingly stringent air pollution control laws, reflecting in part Federal government efforts to foster so-called clean coal technology use, and perhaps in part to declining unit costs for pollution control.

Figure 3: **Fuel shares in electricity output in the US, 1990**

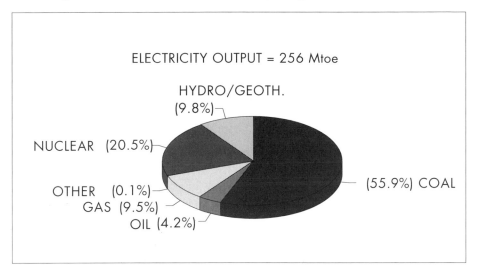

ELECTRICITY OUTPUT = 256 Mtoe

HYDRO/GEOTH.
(9.8%)

NUCLEAR (20.5%)

OTHER (0.1%)
GAS (9.5%)
OIL (4.2%)

(55.9%) COAL

Electricity generation is the dominant use of coal in the United States, accounting for some 84 per cent of total coal consumption. Transformation sector consumption of natural gas (electricity generation, energy production and refining) consumed almost 30 per cent of total gas supply in 1990.

The changes in total final consumption from 1979 to 1990, and the relative shares of TFC for each fuel in 1990, and shown in Figures 4 and 5. Sectoral shares of final consumption are shown in Figure 6.

Final consumption of petroleum products is concentrated in transport, where it is virtually the only primary fuel consumed; consumption in this sector has generally risen regardless of fluctuating oil prices. Non-energy uses of petroleum products account for almost 10 per cent of oil TFC, primarily in industry and in transport.

Industrial use of oil and gas has fluctuated throughout the decade, primarily as a function of industrial output, capital stock turnover and relative fuel prices. U. S. industrial consumers, like the generating sector, have a high degree of fuel switching capability relative to other OECD countries, so that the fuel mix in these two sectors (particularly the shares of oil and gas) show a noticeable response to changing relative fuel prices.

Figure 4: **Total TFC and TFC by fuel in the US, 1979 and 1990**

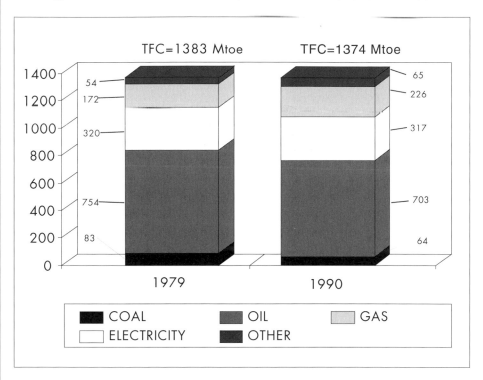

Figure 5: **Fuel shares in TFC in the US, 1990**

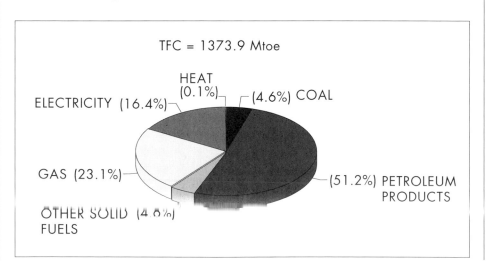

Figure 6: **TFC by sector in the US, 1990**

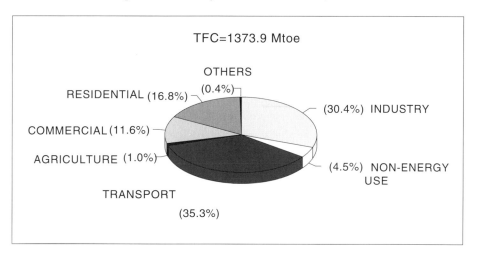

TFC=1373.9 Mtoe

OTHERS (0.4%)

RESIDENTIAL (16.8%)

(30.4%) INDUSTRY

COMMERCIAL (11.6%)

AGRICULTURE (1.0%)

(4.5%) NON-ENERGY USE

TRANSPORT (35.3%)

ENERGY-RELATED POLLUTION PROFILE[3]

Energy-related pollution in the US stems primarily from fuel combustion in two main activities: transport and process heat generation (including electricity production). The primary pollutants that flow from this fuel combustion include CO_2, SO_2, NO_x and particulates. In the past decade, the laws regulating these pollutants have become progressively more stringent, as reflected in reductions - some dramatic - in energy-related emissions.

CO_2 emissions

Annual man-made energy-related CO_2 emissions in the United States rose from 4.9 billion tons in 1980 to 5 billion tons in 1990. In 1990 some 2 billion tons (39 per cent of total emissions) came from electricity generation and refineries; industry accounted for 771 million tons (15 per cent); residential and commercial for 544 million tons (11 per cent). Some 1.5 billion tons (30 per cent) came from mobile sources.

In 1980, by comparison, the transformation sector produced 1.7 billion tons (35 per cent) of CO_2 emissions; industry, 920 million tons (19 per cent); residential and commercial, 637 million tons (13 per cent). Mobile sources accounted for 1.3 billion tons (27 per cent of total emissions) in that year.

Indices relating emissions to economic and population growth show that U.S. emissions of CO_2 per unit of GDP in 1988 were 324kg/US$ 1 000 (1985), while emissions per capita (kg/cap.) were 5.8. The OECD average for these two indices for that year are 286 and 3.4 respectively.

---

3 The statistics for CO_2 used in these Energy-Related Pollution Profiles have been compiled and calculated by the IEA/OECD as current but as yet unpublished updates of the statistics in the *OECD Environmental Data Compendium 1991*, and may not correspond exactly with national statistics. The statistics on other pollutants in US are taken from the *Compendium* and may not correspond with national statistics.

SO$_2$ emissions

Total emissions of SO$_2$ in the United States fell from 23.4 million tons in 1980 to 20.7 in 1988, a drop of 12 per cent. Emissions from stationary sources throughout the decade represent about 96 per cent of total emissions, with mobile sources comprising only a small part.

Efforts to reduce these emissions in the past decade have included some switching to low sulfur fuels (low sulfur coals and fuel oil with less than 0.3 per cent sulfur are required in some areas), installing scrubbers and other SO$_2$ removal technologies, including fluidised bed combustors. These efforts have resulted in a diminution of SO$_2$ emissions, both absolutely and relative to fossil fuel use.

Indices relating SO$_2$ emissions to GDP and to population at the end of the decade of the 1980s show the United States at 4.7 kg/US\$ 1 000 (1985) and 84 kg/cap., versus OECD averages of 4.1 kg/US\$ 1 000 (1985) and 48.3kg/cap.

Concentrations of SO$_2$ (micrograms/m³) in the United States have fallen significantly as a result of emissions reductions, from an index figure of 100 (micrograms/m³) in 1980, to a national average of 76 in 1988, 87 in New York City, 48 in Los Angeles and 74 in Denver.

NO$_x$ emissions

Nitrogen oxide emissions in the United States declined slightly in the last decade, from an all-time high of 20.4 million tons of emissions in 1980 to 19.6 million in 1988. During this time, the contribution of mobile sources to NO$_x$ emissions has fallen from 46 per cent to 41 per cent of total emissions. This reflects a concerted program of emissions control for automobiles, including the widespread introduction of catalytic converters, mitigated by a growth in the number of vehicles and in vehicle use (which has tended to increase numbers of polluters and emissions).

Concentrations of NO$_x$ (micrograms/m³) in selected U.S. cities show varied success in reducing NO$_x$ pollution. With 1980 as the base year, in 1988 index figures for the United States are as follows: national average, 91; New York city, 101; Los Angeles, 83; and Denver, 123.

Indices showing US emissions of NO$_x$ relative to GDP and to population show emissions in 1988 of 4.5 kg/US\$ 1 000 (1985) of GDP, and 80.4 kg/cap. The OECD average for these indices was 3.8 kg/US$ 1 000 (1985) GDP, and 44.3 kg/cap.

Particulates

U.S. particulate emissions levels reflect successful control technologies, having dropped from 8.5 million tons in 1980 to 6.9 million in 1988. In 1988, some 80 per cent of particulate emissions came from stationary sources, down from 85 per cent in 1980.

This decline in particulates emissions is reflected in a drop in particulates concentrations (micrograms/m³). The national average concentration fell from an index base of 100 (micrograms/m³) in 1980 to 79 in 1988. Progress in major cities was varied, with 1988 concentrations in New York falling to 88, in Los Angeles to 93, in Denver to 70 and in Mesa Verde to 53, all measured against the same index base.

PART II
ENERGY TAXES
AS POLICY MEASURES
IN THE CASE
STUDY COUNTRIES

INTRODUCTION TO PART II

Taxes can serve many purposes. Taxes levied for one purpose might ultimately also be found useful for policy reasons which did not even exist when the tax was originally imposed. One of the purposes of this section is to review the evolution of energy taxation, and explore the degree to which taxes already in place can serve different policy goals.

Energy has mostly been taxed because it is convenient to tax. Energy is necessary to maintain modern society as we know it, providing a broad and somewhat inelastic tax base for an easily administered tax. For governments taxing to raise revenues, energy consumption offers an especially excellent vehicle. Perhaps no other motives than this have led to existing energy consumption taxes. Nevertheless, over time, some of the effects of consumption and production-related energy taxes (income redistribution, capture of rents, lower consumption, changes in fuel mix) have become important in their own right. Both fiscal and other policies have thus been served by energy taxes not imposed to do so.

It is thus important to distinguish here between a tax levied on energy consumption and a tax levied to change energy consumption. Most energy taxes are of the former variety. The section on Taxing to Change Consumption/Energy Security will explore the potential application of these same taxes to change patterns of energy use.

It would also be helpful to remember in the discussion that follows, that the absolute level of an energy tax (along with price elasticity of demand or supply) determines the revenues to be gained. This is important where revenue raising is the goal. The relative level of taxes on different fuels or on different energy uses can also affect relative costs, which will determine fuel use choices. This can have competitive implications for fuel suppliers and for consuming industries, and is relevant where energy taxes are levied to promote energy security or environmental goals. Moreover, distribution of revenues from an energy tax can be every bit as important to the effect of the tax as the level and incidence of the tax itself. These questions are relevant particularly where energy taxes are being considered for environmental purposes.

Part II reviews energy taxes in the five case study countries to see how their effects might be applied in three areas: fiscal policy, energy policy and environmental concerns. The discussion is confined to a factual comparison of the case studies; theoretical and policy issues will be explored in the next and last Part. The discussion here is guided by two questions: "To what end is an energy tax being used?" and "How effectively is the tax designed to achieve this end?"

The following sections first explore energy taxes as fiscal measures: for raising revenues, redistributing income and capturing rent (a special case of redistributing income); and second, the uses of energy taxes for other than fiscal purposes. This latter, more recent approach uses tax-induced price increases primarily as incentives to reduce energy consumption, to serve such non-fiscal policies as security of energy supply and environmental protection.

ENERGY TAXES AS FISCAL MEASURES

Raising revenues

In the case study countries, energy taxes have historically been used to raise revenues, with motor fuels the principal target. Taxes on motor fuels alone accounted for 1.6 per cent of the national government's fiscal revenues in the United States in 1990, 2 per cent in Denmark, 3.7 per cent in Japan, 4.8 per cent in Germany, and 6 per cent in Australia.

Motor fuels are almost universally taxed, in part because of the historical assumption that demand is fairly inelastic. Table 1 shows the relative importance of consumption taxes in the final price of motor fuels in the five case study countries, as calculated by the IEA in *Energy Prices and Taxes*, Fourth Quarter, 1991. The range is broad, with the United States lowest in the OECD for any given fuel and Germany the highest among the case study countries.

Table 1. **National taxes on motor fuels as per cent of final price**
(per toe 1991, in national currencies)

	Price including tax	Tax	Tax as % of final price
Australia (A$)			
Leaded premium	.586	.311	53%
Unleaded premium	.634	.311	49%
Unleaded regular	.586	.311	53%
Diesel	.573	.315	55%
Denmark (DKr)			
Leaded premium	6.057	4.104	68%
Unleaded premium	5.598	3.374	60%
Unleaded regular	5.238	3.302	63%
Diesel	2.653	.555	21%
Germany (DM)			
Leaded premium	1.438	.972	68%
Unleaded premium	1.323	.873	66%
Unleaded regular	1.273	.866	68%
Diesel	.936	.494	53%
Japan (1000 yen)			
Leaded premium	-	-	-
Unleaded premium	-	-	-
Unleaded regular	0.127	0.058	46%
Diesel	0.077	0.027	35%
United States (US$)			
Leaded premium	NA		
Unleaded premium	.349	.108	31%
Unleaded regular	.301	.099	33%
Diesel	.299	.102	34%

Note that local taxes on motor fuels in the United States comprise a significant and major component of the over-all tax burden. State taxes on gasoline in the U.S. range from 8 cents per gallon in Alaska, to 30 cents per gallon in Connecticut. Total state revenues from motor fuel taxes in 1991 were an estimated US$ 21 billion (vs. US$ 17 billion in federal excises). To the extent that most statistics cite only national, i.e., federal taxes, they tend to underestimate considerably the total U.S. energy-related tax burden on motor fuels.

The total revenues raised by various energy-consumption related taxes in the case study countries for 1991 ranged from 2 per cent of total tax revenues for the United States to 7 per cent in Germany and 7 per cent in Australia (8.6 per cent with motor vehicle taxes, and 10.3 per cent with producer excise taxes). Note that these are gross figures, and may overstate the contribution of energy to national revenues. In some countries, for example, royalty payments and some energy tax payments are deductible from income and other taxes.

Revenues collected from energy taxes may be diminished when large categories of fuel users are energy-tax exempt, or if only one of several available fuels (oil, for example) is taxed, and switching to alternate fuels provides a means of tax avoidance. This is also true where differentiated energy taxes alter relative fuel prices; the capability for fuel switching in this instance would likely result in lower revenues and an altered fuel mix. Present energy taxes, however, generally are not structured to alter relative fuel prices nor set at rates which would do so. The differentiated fuel taxes in the case study countries have been varied for reasons of revenue redistribution or out of concern for competitive industry positions, but (except perhaps for some leaded fuel excises) have not been consciously designed to change consumption behaviour.

Differentiated energy tax rates for Germany (see Part I) are therefore probably successful for raising revenues in part because fuel switching possibilities there tend to be somewhat limited. The government can capitalize on relatively inelastic short run demand and on a fairly rigid fuel use infrastructure to raise revenues from differentiated energy taxes without engendering major fuel shifts as a means of tax avoidance. In the long run, however, differentiated taxes can encourage fuel use flexibility.

Table 2 shows the application of taxes to different energy forms and users, as well as the importance of consumption taxes (VAT and excise taxes) in final energy prices in the five case study countries, as calculated by the IEA in *Energy Prices and Taxes*, Fourth Quarter, 1991. In general, oil products are taxed more heavily than other fuels, though the tax portion of the final price for petroleum products varies among countries and especially among consumer classes.

Table 2. **National taxes as per cent of final energy price in various consuming sectors, on heat equivalent basis**

(per toe or kwh 1991, in national currencies)

Country and Fuel	Households	Electricity Generation	Industry
Australia (A$)			
Light fuel oil	NA		NA
Heavy fuel oil		NA	NA
Natural gas	0	0	0
Steam coal		0	0
Electricity (kWh)	0		0
Denmark (DKr)			
Light fuel oil	60		0
Heavy fuel oil		0	0
Natural gas	18	0	0
Steam coal		0	0
Electricity (kWh)	53		0
Germany (DM)			
Light fuel oil	26		15
Heavy fuel oil		23	13
Natural gas (1990)	17	12	10
Steam coal		0	0
Electricity (kWh)	19		8
Japan (1000 yen)			
Light fuel oil	3		3
Heavy fuel oil		3	3
Natural gas (1990)	3	5	3
Steam coal		3	4
Electricity (kWh) (1990)	5.6		5.5
United States (US$)			
Light fuel oil	5		0
Heavy fuel oil		0	0
Natural gas	0	0	0
Steam coal (1990)		0	0
Electricity (kWh)	0		

Japan and Germany have the broadest energy consumption tax bases, under which several different classes of consumers and most fuels are subject to taxation. Both countries, along with Australia, tax some fuels used for electricity generation and some fuels used for industrial consumption. As of January 1993, Denmark will levy a CO_2-related tax, but not an energy tax, on certain industrial fuel uses, but with full rebates available.

By contrast, all countries tax household consumption of at least some fuels. At a minimum, the United States taxes some light fuel oil at the Federal level, at a nominal rate of a few cents/barrel. At the other end of the range, Japan taxes all household energy use including coal, at a nominal rate of 3 per cent (5.6 percent for electricity). In between, Australia taxes residential use of diesel, kerosene and heating oil; Denmark and Germany tax household consumption of light fuel oil, natural gas and electricity, at rates between 17 and 60 per cent of the final price.

Redistributing income

All five case study countries achieve some modicum of income redistribution through tax forgiveness and subsidies to energy related activities. The most dramatic income redistribution effected in the case study countries through energy taxes is found in the coal subsidies in Germany and Japan.

Subsidies for German hard coal production are provided directly through government payments and indirectly through price supports - cross subsidies by electricity and steel consumers. They are funded in large part by a tax on electricity; revenues transferred to coal mining regions from electricity consumers to coal producers in 1990 amounted to some DM 6 billion, rising to DM 7.6 billion in 1991. Total subsidies to the hard coal industry for 1991 have been estimated by the IEA at DM 22 billion (not quite 2 per cent of total tax revenues).

Japan also subsidises coal production through price supports and by direct grants to producers. Price supports in the form of cross-subsidies from the electricity sector are estimated by the IEA to be 109 billion Yen for FY 1990/91 and 103 billion for FY 1991/92. Direct government aid is financed in large measure through customs duties levied on crude oil imports, earmarked to a special coal industry support fund. IEA estimates of total assistance to the Japanese coal industry for FY 1990/91 is

213 billion Yen, or 0.3 per cent of total tax revenues. For FY 1991/92, total support fell to 200 billion Yen.

Capturing rents

Capturing rents is a special case of income redistribution among different groups in society and over time. There is no single most efficient distribution of rents. Governments have traditionally collected rents from natural resource (including energy) development, using royalties, straight revenue sharing license agreements, government participation schemes, and taxes. Each of these measures will have different effects on investment and production decisions.

Taxes on energy production are used explicitly to capture rents only in Australia and Denmark among the case study countries. Both countries levy profits-based (or windfall profits) taxes on hydrocarbon production (and until recently, in Australia on coal). Denmark uses the hydrocarbon tax scheme to tax profits stemming from world crude oil price changes. A company's price related profits amounting to more than 25 per cent of its oil- and gas-related investment is subject to a tax of 70 per cent (vs 34-38 per cent for other income). This scheme has partly (although perhaps not explicitly) replaced royalties in Denmark. It is seen as more flexible and conducive to investment and production under a variety of market conditions.

Revenues from the hydrocarbon tax in 1990 were DKr 486 million; royalties from oil and gas production were DKr 633 million.

In Australia, the crude oil excise tax was explicitly devised to capture rents associated with world oil price increases in the 1970s and '80s. The tax was imposed as part of a larger price control and allocation scheme whereby the Commonwealth instead of domestic producers captured the gains from the price increases. The United States, it should be noted, instituted a similar price control and allocation scheme in that same period, but without the tax.

Australia also has a profits-based producer tax explicitly designed to replace royalties, called the Petroleum Resource Rent Tax (PRRT). This scheme was designed primarily to govern the distribution of industry/government gains in the Bass Strait without discouraging investment or production, when it became clear that the area would become a major hydrocarbon producer. The PRRT is in principle applicable to other areas, and has its analogies at the state level. Where it is applied, the

PRRT replaces both royalties and the producer excise tax. Like the Danish hydrocarbon tax, the PRRT has the benefit of flexibility and creates relatively few distortions in producer/investor incentives.

In FY 1991/92, revenues from these producer taxes amounted to A$ 293 million for the PRRT and A$ 1.35 billion for the excise tax, accounting for some 1.7 per cent of total tax revenues. Royalties that year accounted for a maximum of A$ 337 million.

Governments have also used consumption taxes, including excise taxes on energy, to capture consumer surplus made evident by market or producer price fluctuations. Since the 1970s, several European countries in particular have used both fluctuating and relatively high energy taxes, particularly on motor fuels, to even out price fluctuations and often to capture rents. This pricing/tax policy is also credited with having reduced energy consumption, and its continued practice is one example of how energy taxes have evolved from fiscal measures to incentive taxes.

ENERGY TAXES AS
NON-FISCAL POLICY MEASURES

Taxing to reduce consumption

A major importance of the oil price increases in the 1970's is that they weakened both the conceptual linkage between energy use and economic growth, and the assumption of inelastic oil and energy demand. The use of energy consumption taxes to influence energy demand thus became politically possible. High energy prices (at least partly tax-induced and certainly in some cases tax-maintained) are now seen as having the potential to reduce energy consumption and encourage more efficient energy use, without necessarily sacrificing economic growth.

Figures 1-3 show gains in energy efficiency in the case study countries since 1980, as calculated by the IEA and measured as TPES/GDP, consumption per capita, and industrial consumption/industrial output. Note, however, that these figures show total changes and do not indicate fluctuations throughout the course of the decade.

Energy consumption has been growing in Australia and in Japan, but falling in the other case study countries; population and GDP have grown in all countries. Nevertheless, the efficiency of energy use in all of these economies (TPES/GDP) has improved, along with energy use per capita, in every country but Australia and Japan. Japan and Denmark have among the lowest energy intensities (TPES/GDP) in the OECD.

These improvements in energy efficiency reflect and have been mitigated by a number of countervailing trends. Improved fuel efficiency of cars has been off-set by the effects of a growing population and more driving; growing affluence has led to growth in home size and central heating, but also to more insulation.

Energy efficiency in industry has improved in the same time frame, expressed as a decline in the ratio of industrial energy consumption/industrial production. In some countries, like Australia, over-all industrial efficiency gains have been masked by the expansion of energy-intensive industries.

Figure 1: **Change in TPES/GDP***

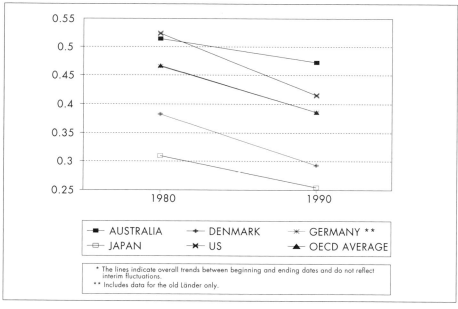

Figure 2: **Change in per capita energy consumption***

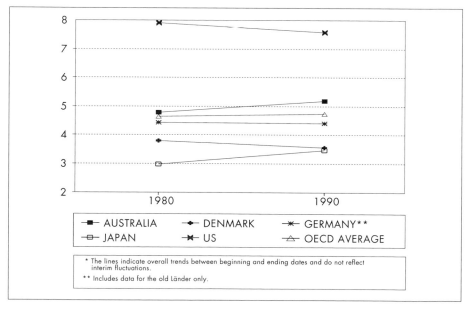

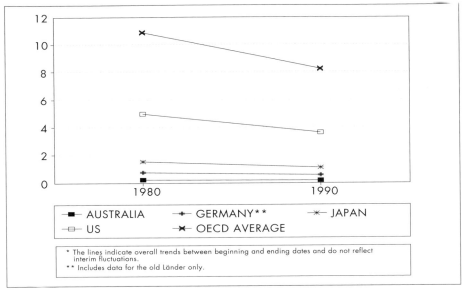

Figure 3: **Change in industrial energy consumption/
industrial production index***

* The lines indicate overall trends between beginning and ending dates and do not reflect
interim fluctuations.
** Includes data for the old Länder only.

The ratios of energy intensity, calculated by the IEA and shown here for Germany, could only be calculated for the old Länder. Comparisons of energy intensity over time for all of Germany are only possible on a per capita basis, using separate data for each region as provided by the German government. These figures show per capita energy consumption (TPES/cap.) for the new Länder falling from 5.1 toe/cap. in 1980 to 4.52 in 1990. Comparable figures for the old Länder show energy consumption (TPES/cap.) in that region falling slightly, from 4.44 toe/cap. in 1980 to 4.35 in 1990.

Efficiency gains in the industrial sector in Germany are also only available for the old Länder, as shown in Figure 3. In the new Länder, industrial gains in energy efficiency are initially expected to result from changes in energy prices, and over time from new technologies and investment.

Not all of the above efficiency gains can be attributed to price effects, much less to tax-induced price effects, though the former unarguably played a major role, and served as an impetus for governments to take non-price-related actions to reinforce improvements in energy efficiency. However, the experience of the 1970s highlights the potential for reduced energy consumption through responses to price changes in markets previously thought to be highly inelastic.

Energy taxes are increasingly being re-examined in this new context. There is a continued and growing interest in the use of energy taxes to create incentives for reducing energy consumption, often as an intermediate step to accomplishing other policy goals. The OECD and the IEA are exploring the application of energy taxes as economic instruments to further policy goals in a number of areas[1]. The discussion here will focus on two such policy areas of primary interest to the IEA, energy security and the environment.

A cautionary digression is in order, however, before proceeding with that discussion. While demand for energy is relatively inelastic in the short run, the price elasticity of energy demand in the long run tends to be higher. Capital turnover permits adjustment to long term changes in energy prices. Thus investments have been made in energy saving technologies in response to world oil and other energy price increases in the 1970's. Over the last decade, however, the real cost of energy has been falling in important sectors (see Figures 4-9).

Figure 4: **Real price indices for industry in Germany**

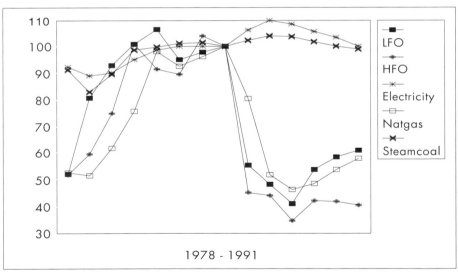

1978 - 1991

1. Some of the work already published includes :
"Energy and the Environment : Policy Overview", IEA, 1989;
"Greenhouse Gas Emission, the Energy Dimension", OECD/IEA, 1991, Paris;
"A Survey of Studies of the Costs of Reducing Greenhouse Gas Emissions", Department of Economics and Statistics Working Paper N°.89, Paris, OECD (1990);
"Recent Developments in the Use of Economic Instruments for Environmental Protection"; Environment Monograph N°.41, OECD (1991), Paris;
"Energy Prices, Taxes and Carbon Dioxide Emissions", Department of Economics and Statistics, Working Paper N°. 106, OECD (1991), Paris;
"Environmental Policy : How to Apply Economic Instruments", OECD (1991), Paris.

Figure 5: **Real price indices for industry in Japan**

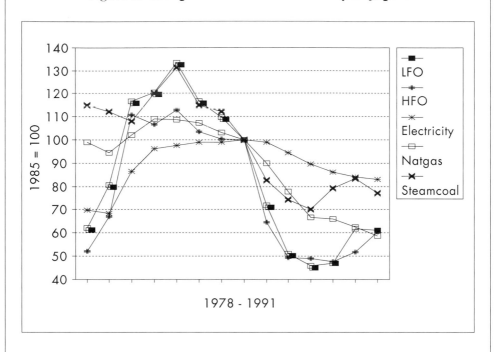

Figure 6: **Real price indices for industry in the USA**

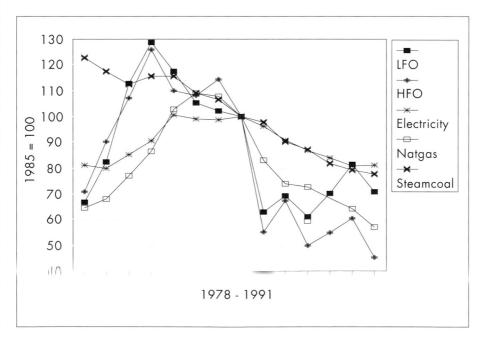

Figure 7: **Real price indices for households in Germany**

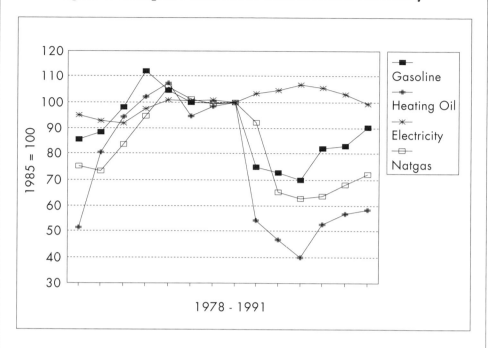

Figure 8: **Real price indices for households in Japan**

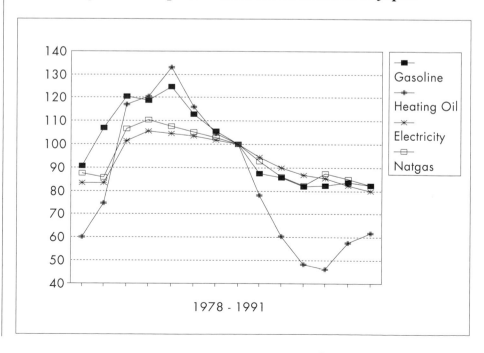

Figure 9: **Real price indices for households in the US**

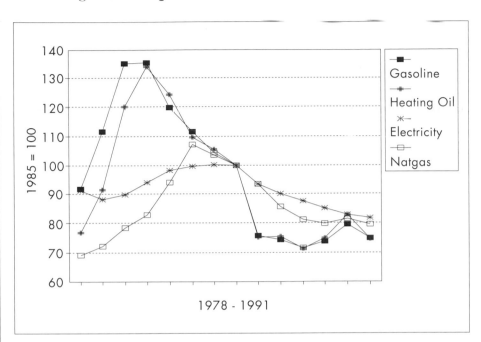

Figure 9: **Real price indices for households in the US**

Moreover, according to unpublished cost studies by major manufac-turers of energy-related pollution control technologies (SO_2 and NO_x removal), the real cost of such technologies has also declined in the last decade by some 10-50 percent, allowing for design changes and depending on technology and manufacturer.

One could infer two things from this. The first is that the real cost of cleaner energy has been falling, at least in some sectors. One would expect capital investment to reflect these circumstances. Efforts to reduce energy use through tax-induced price increases will need to consider, and will have attendant implications for, investment in infrastructure. Governments may choose to use energy taxes to counter-act the effects of falling (clean) energy prices in some sectors, and so to slow the pace of investment in energy-using technologies. Leaving aside any moral value that may be attached to using less energy, it is good to bear in mind that inefficient energy conservation, that goes beyond proper internalisation of externalities can also exist, and that it can have a real cost to society. Energy taxation aimed at influencing long term investment without regard for this fact runs the risk of creating serious inefficiencies and distortions.

The second is that the remaining externalities associated with certain kinds of energy-related pollution, and the costs of energy-related pollution abatement are being increasingly internalised and reduced. Increasingly efficient and less costly pollution control represents a certain level of internalisation of energy-related pollution costs, as do gains in the efficiency of energy use. Historical damage figures may thus over-state the level of future externalities remaining to be internalised through a tax, for example, and this should be considered in efforts to design efficient pollution-related energy taxes.

According to IEA and OECD estimates made in the context of analysing greenhouse gas emissions control, tax levels required to induce large reductions in energy demand for whatever reason are likely to be high[2]. Depending on the target sectors and on the target level of conservation, the short-run elasticity of energy demand may be too low to permit large-scale energy conservation in the adjustment period, or the tax level required may be too high to permit even long-term adjustments without serious economic distortions. In the case study countries (assuming a continuation of present trends and conditions), energy taxes would have to be increased regularly and consistently over time to achieve any major conservation effect.

Taxing to change consumption/energy security

OECD countries have a continuing concern about security of energy supply, which can be defined in a number of ways. (See IEA/SLT document (87) 38, "Government Market Interventions - An Oil Import Fee"). These include energy security defined as self-sufficiency, wartime capability, minimisation of adjustment lags, reduced import dependency (especially oil imports), and price stability. For purposes of this discussion we will consider the two principal definitions used by the IEA: reduced oil dependence and responsive energy markets.

---

2. For example, according to work described in *"An Analysis of Energy Policy Measures and Their Impact on CO_2 Emission"*, IEA, Paris, June 1991, a carbon tax of US$100/t carbon imposed on energy from 1991 would result in an OECD-wide reduction of energy consumption from base line projections of 6.8% in 1995 and 7.4% in 2005.

In the aftermath of the oil price rises of the 1970s, OECD countries made serious efforts to reduce their oil consumption and their strategic vulnerability to market turmoil. Figures 10 and 11 show the results of these efforts, which effectively reduced oil intensity (sometimes dramatically), in all sectors but transport, and generally more than the reductions achieved in the same period for total energy intensity. Again note that figures show changes from 1980 to 1990, and do not reflect intervening fluctuations.

Figure 10: **Change in oil supply per unit of GDP***

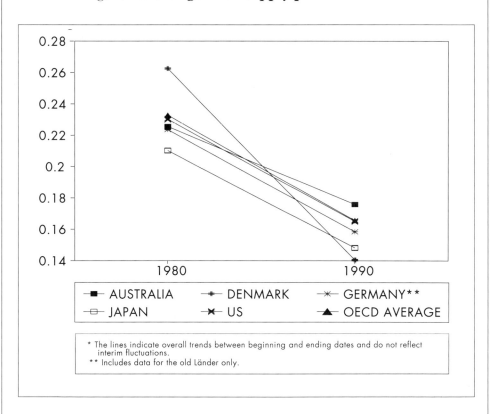

* The lines indicate overall trends between beginning and ending dates and do not reflect interim fluctuations.
** Includes data for the old Länder only.

If energy security is defined in terms of reduced oil dependence and if governments opt for energy taxes as a policy tool, they might tax oil or imported oil, to make it relatively more expensive than other fuels. Taxes on oil products to reduce consumption imply a conservation effect as well as a fuel switching effect. How much each obtains depends on the elasticity of oil demand in each sector, the elasticity of over-all energy demand, and the technological and economic capabilities for fuel switching. Governments might also promote fuel switching by using differentiated energy taxes to alter relative fuel prices over time (perhaps in favour of domestic energy resources, though this is not necessarily efficient).

Figure 11: **Change in industry oil consumption/ industrial production index***

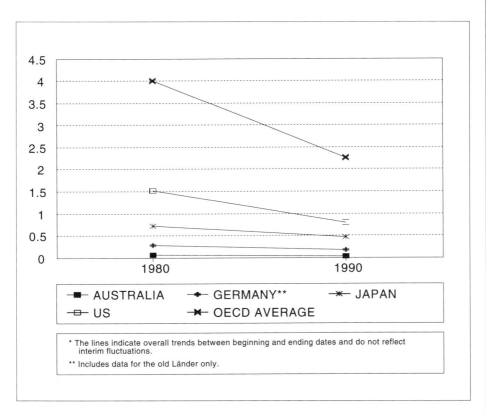

* The lines indicate overall trends between beginning and ending dates and do not reflect interim fluctuations.

** Includes data for the old Länder only.

Have countries already used energy taxes in this way for energy security purposes? Or have they largely been satisfied with the consumption effects of market price movements and parallel efficiency gains? Could existing taxes be used to this end?

Motor fuel taxes are clearly adaptable to foster energy conservation (and some fuel switching in the longer term) even though they were not structured to this end and notwithstanding their present levels. Motor fuels account for somewhere between 39 and 70 per cent of oil consumption in the case study countries, with Australia and the United States having the highest share (70 and 64 per cent respectively). This is not surprising given the high percentage of coal- and not oil-fired electricity generation in these countries and their respective infrastructures. In Japan, motor fuels represent a much lower share of total oil requirements (39 per cent), reflecting a higher use of oil for electricity generation and boiler fuel.

All else being equal, and depending on elasticities and possibilities for substitution, the higher the share of taxes in final price, the higher the incremental tax required to produce a given incremental result. The United States, for example, taxes motor fuels at the national level at rates considerably lower than the other case study countries, but this does not necessarily mean it should raise its rates to levels prevailing in other case study countries to achieve a given reduction in consumption. Given the elasticity of demand for motor fuels in the U. S. and the transparency of prices, even a small increase in taxes could be expected to elicit a relatively larger reduction in consumption in the U. S. market than the same tax might do in European markets. These differences in tax levels, relative tax/price ratios and tax bases, also have implications for proposals to increase motor fuels taxes aimed at changing behaviour, particularly if they envisage harmonisation or coordination of taxes among countries, as discussed in Part III.

At present, only household use of motor fuels and fuel oil, among oil products, are taxed in all five case study countries. Other uses of oil such as electricity generation and industrial use, which could also be taxed to reduce consumption or to encourage fuel switching, are only taxed in Australia, Japan and Germany. And in Germany, fuel oil, even though taxed in all sectors, is still cheaper than alternate fuels in all consuming sectors. Moreover, the high prices maintained for substitute fuels (coal and gas) in European markets may limit some of the immediate attractiveness of fuel switching.

Excise taxes in Denmark and Germany (and less transparently in Japan) which fund emergency petroleum storage are also used to further the goal of energy supply security, defined in terms of reduced oil import dependence. While storage does not directly reduce dependence on oil or oil imports, the strategic reserves can cushion short-term market disruptions.

The second interpretation of energy security holds that responsive energy markets provide the best security of energy supply. Market responsiveness tends to be diminished to the extent that taxation is used as a tool for price stabilisation. Price stabilization policies have tended to limit the market response potential in European countries and in Japan relative to countries like the U.S., where responses to market and price fluctuations are left more to the markets.

Taxing to reduce energy-consumption-related pollution

The reader should note at the outset of this discussion that the use of the term energy-related pollution in this study refers to a number of kinds of air pollution, including sulfur dioxide and nitrogen oxides and particulates, as well as CO_2 and also treats briefly land and water pollution. The focus of this paper is determinedly on existing taxes and their adaptability to new policy situations. It does not suggest a remedy for greenhouse gas and CO_2 emissions, though these are treated as relevant, and form part of the discussions in Part III on harmonisation, competition, and the appropriateness of using energy taxes as a tool for reducing global vs. local pollution.

Governments have begun to evaluate energy taxes for their potential to reduce energy-related pollution, particularly air pollution from energy combustion. Taxing energy is assumed to raise the cost of energy and so reduce consumption, along with consumption-related pollution. Whether energy taxes are an efficient incentive for reducing pollution is explored more fully in Part III. Of interest here is whether existing energy taxes can be used as a vehicle for taxing polluters.

Tables 3 - 7 display graphically the combined tax/energy/pollution profile of each case study country, allowing one to see which energy users and which polluters are subject to energy taxes. These combined profiles show that heavy fuel users, heavy polluters, and fuels with a high polluting potential, are seldomly and/or lightly taxed. There is, in some cases, almost an inverse relationship between pollution emissions and energy tax burden.

Table 3. **Australia (1990)**

ENERGY		EMISSIONS				ENERGY TAXES[2]
		CO$_2$[1]	SO$_2$	NO$_x$	PARTICULATES	
		TOTALS				
TPES	89 mtoe	274	80	261	NA	
Coal	40%					
Oil	37%					
Gas	17%					
Other[3]	6%					
CONSUMING SECTORS		SECTORAL SHARES				
Stationary sources, of which		206.3	71	60	NA	
Electricity Generation		128[6]	27	29	NA	
Input	35 mtoe					
Output	13 mtoe					
Coal	77%					No
Oil	3%					Yes
Gas	11%					No
Other[3]	10%					No

Industry	24 mtoe	45.9	44	NA	NA
Coal	17%				No
Oil	26%				Yes
Gas	27%				No
Electricity	21%				No
Other[4]	10%				No
Households and other[5]	12 mtoe	8.3	NA	NA	NA
Coal	1%				No
Oil	15%				Yes
Gas	22%				No
Electricity	48%				No
Other[4]	14%				No
Mobile sources					
Transport	23 mtoe	67.7	8.8	201	20
Gasoline	1%				Yes
Diesel	15%				Yes[7]
Total Final Consumption	59 mtoe				

1. In million tons of CO_2 for 1990; all other emissions in 1 000 tons: SO_2, and NO_x emissions for 8 major cities only, for 1985; particulates for mobile sources only, for 1987–88.
2. Federal taxes only.
3. Other = hydro, geothermal, electricity trade, other.
4. Other = heat, other.
5. Includes residential, commercial, public service and agricultural sectors.
6. Emissions figure includes all energy transformation including refineries.
7. Includes partial rebates to commercial and industrial users.

Table 4. **Denmark (1990)**

ENERGY		EMISSIONS				ENERGY TAXES
		CO$_2$[1]	SO$_2$	NO$_x$	PARTICULATES	
		TOTALS				
TPES	18.3 mtoe	56.3	193	249	NA	
Coal	33%					
Oil	48%					
Gas	10%					
Other[2]	10%					
CONSUMING SECTORS		SECTORAL SHARES				
Stationary sources, of which		39.4	182	160	NA	
Electricity Generation		25.2[5]	NA	NA	NA	
Input	6.7 mtoe					
Output	2.2 mtoe					
Coal	91%					No
Oil	4%					No
Gas	2%					NA
Other[3]	3%					No

Industry	2.8 mtoe	6.55	NA	NA	NA	No
Coal	10%					No
Oil	45%					No
Gas	17%					No
Electricity	24%					No
Other[3]	5%				NA	NA
Households and other[4]	5.7 mtoe	6	NA	NA	NA	
Coal	1%					Yes
Oil	36%					Yes
Gas	11%					Yes
Electricity	31%					Yes
Other[3]	17%				NA	NA
Mobile sources						
Transport	4.6 mtoe	16.9	11	89	4	
Gasoline	1%					Yes
Diesel	15%					Yes[6]
Total Final Consumption	13.1 mtoe					

1. In million tons of CO_2 for 1990; all other emissions in 1 000, tons. 1989 for SO_2, and 1988 for NO_x
2. Other = hydro, geothermal, electricity trade, other.
3. Other = heat, other.
4. Includes residential, commercial, public service and agricultural sectors.
5. Emissions figure includes all energy transformation including refineries.
6. Includes partial rebates to commercial and industrial users.

Table 5. **Germany (1990)**

ENERGY		EMISSIONS (1989)				ENERGY TAXES[2]
		CO$_2$[1]	SO$_2$	NO$_x$	PARTICULATES	
		TOTALS				
TPES	278 mtoe	1040	5 595	3 210	2 171	
Coal	27%					
Oil	41%					
Gas	17%					
Other[3]	15%					
CONSUMING SECTORS		SECTORAL SHARES				
Stationary sources, of which			5 475	1 040	2 064	
Electricity Generation		374[6]	4 070	610	1 075	
Input	108 mtoe					
Output	39 mtoe					
Coal	52%					No
Oil	2%					Yes
Gas	8%					NA
Other[3]	38%					No

Industry	72 mtoe	126	810	310	568	
Coal	22%					No
Oil	34%					Yes
Gas	22%					Yes
Electricity	22%					Yes
Other[4]	–					NA
Households and other[5]	72 mtoe	201	595	120	241	
Coal	3%					No
Oil	43%					Yes
Gas	27%					Yes
Electricity	23%					Yes
Other[4]	5%					NA
Mobile sources						
Transport	53 mtoe	181	120	2 170	107	
Gasoline						Yes
Diesel						Yes[7]
Total Final Consumption	197 mtoe					

1. Million of tons of CO_2 for 1990; all other emissions in 1 000 tons.
2. Federal taxes only.
3. Other = nuclear (38%), hydro, geothermal, electricity trade, other.
4. Other = heat, other.
5. Includes residential, commercial, public service and agricultural sectors.
6. Emissions figure includes all energy transformation including refineries and extractive mining.
7. Includes partial rebates to commercial and industrial users.

Table 6. **Japan (1990)**

ENERGY		EMISSIONS				ENERGY TAXES[2]
		CO$_2$[1]	SO$_2$ (1986)	NO$_x$(1986)	PARTICULATES	
			TOTALS			
TPES	428 mtoe	1060	835	1 176	NA	
Coal	17%					
Oil	58%					
Gas	10%					
Other[3]	15%					
CONSUMING SECTORS			SECTORAL SHARES			
Stationary sources, of which		843	684	662	NA	
Electricity Generation		351[6]	173	167	NA	
Input	170 mtoe					
Output	73 mtoe					
Coal	14%					Yes[7]
Oil	32%					Yes
Gas	19%					Yes
Other[3]	35%					Yes

Industry	149 mtoe	179	NA	NA	NA	NA
Coal	26%					No
Oil	46%					Yes
Gas	3%					Yes
Electricity	25%					Yes
Other[4]	0%					-
Households and other[5]	79 mtoe	94.1	NA	NA	NA	NA
Coal	.1%					Yes[7]
Oil	43%					Yes
Gas	10%					Yes
Electricity	26%					Yes
Other[4]	.2%					No
Mobile sources						
Transport	70 mtoe	217	151	514	NA	NA
Gasoline						Yes
Diesel						Yes
Total Final Consumption	298 mtoe					

1. In million tons of CO_2 for 1990; all other emissions in 1 000 tons.
2. Federal taxes only.
3. Other = nuclear (24%), hydro, geothermal, other.
4. Other = heat, other.
5. Includes residential, commercial, public service and agricultural sectors.
6. Emissions figure includes all energy transformation including refineries.
7. Consumption tax only.

Table 7. **United States (1990)**

ENERGY		EMISSIONS				ENERGY TAXES[2]
		CO₂[1]	SO₂	NOₓ	PARTICULATES	
		TOTALS				
TPES	1 906 mtoe	5030	20 700	19 800	6 900	
Coal	24%					
Oil	40%					
Gas	23%					
Othe	13%					
CONSUMING SECTORS		SECTORAL SHARES				
Stationary sources, of which		3520	19 800	11 700	5 500	
Electric ty Generation		1770[6]	NA	NA	NA	
Inpu	672 mtoe					
Outp t	256 mtoe					
Coal	56%					No
Oil	4%					No
Gas	10%					SLT
Other	30%					No

Industry	479 mtoe	771	NA	NA	NA	
Coal	12%					No
Oil	32%					No
Gas	32%					SLT
Electricity	15%					SLT
Other[4]	9%					No
Households and other[5]	409 mtoe	544	NA	NA	NA	
Coal	2%					No
Oil	16%					SLT
Gas	40%					SLT
Electricity	37%					SLT
Other[4]	5%					No
Mobile sources						
Transport	485 mtoe	1510	952	8 180	1 400	
Gasoline						Yes
Diesel						Yes
Total Final Consumption	1 373 mtoe					

1. In million tons of CO$_2$ for 1990; all other emissions in 1 000 tons , for 1988.
2. Federal taxes only. "SLT" indicates state and/or local taxes may apply.
3. Other = hydro, geothermal, electricity trade, other.
4. Other = heat, other.
5. Includes residential, commercial, public service and agricultural sectors.
6. Emissions figure includes all energy transformation including refineries.

In Australia, 75 per cent of CO_2 emissions come from stationary sources, including 47 per cent from power generation, fuelled mostly by coal. Coal use is not taxed. In fact, only oil and petroleum products are taxed, accounting for some 14 per cent of total energy consumption among stationary sources. Sulfur dioxide emissions stem mostly (84 per cent) from power generation, yet only the 3 per cent of generating mix that is oil is taxed. By contrast, motor fuel, which causes 79 per cent of NO_x emissions is subject to motor fuel excise taxes.

In Denmark, electricity generation, which contributes almost half of total CO_2 emissions, is not taxed at all; its inputs are not even subject to the CO_2-related tax. Industrial fuel use is also exempt from energy taxes and is eligible for rebates of the CO_2-related tax. As for SO_2 and NO_x, stationary sources account respectively for 94 and 65 per cent of emissions, yet fuel use in these sectors, except for households, is not taxed. And in the "household and others" sector, only households and not commercial, public service or agricultural uses are taxed. The proportion of energy and pollution that is actually taxed in this overall sector is thus considerably less than indicated by the figures in Table 4.

In Germany, stationary sources including electricity generation, account for 90 per cent of fuel use, 83 per cent of CO_2 emissions, 93 per cent of SO_2, 32 per cent of NO_x, and 80 per cent of particulates. Yet coal, which provides 30 per cent of this fuel, and presumably at least that much in emissions, is not taxed in any sector; in fact, its use is subsidised. Germany does, however, tax industrial use of oil, gas and electricity, and the use of oil for power generation, though this is minimal.

Japan has the broadest energy tax base of all the case study countries. In Japan, stationary sources account for 80 per cent of fuel consumption and produce 81 per cent of CO_2 emissions, 82 per cent of SO_2 , and 56 per cent of NO_x. Japan levies taxes on virtually all fuels and on most stationary source uses, although the level of tax is low in most instances. Mobile sources, accounting for 15 per cent of total energy use, are also taxed. These sources account for 20 per cent of CO_2 emissions, 18 per cent of SO_2, 44 per cent of NO_x.

In the United States, except for state and local taxes, virtually no taxes are levied on energy use by stationary sources. Fuel use accounting for some 70 per cent of CO_2 emissions, 26 per cent of SO_2, 59 per cent of NO_x, and 80 per cent of particulates, is thus not taxed at the national level. Mobile sources are generally taxed through motor fuels excises.

In light of the above, it is clear that substantial reductions in energy-related pollution are not likely to be achieved merely through increases in present energy tax rates. Changes in tax base and structure and in policy orientation are needed if energy taxes are to be used effectively as tools to reduce pollution or to implement environmental policies.

Whether and how such restructuring should take place is a policy choice for each individual government. However, governments that do opt for a more environmentally-oriented energy tax regime need to do so in a balanced context. Some of the issues to be addressed in this regard are the focus of Part III.

PART III
DEFINITIONS
AND CHOICES
FOR ENERGY TAX
REFORM

INTRODUCTION TO PART III

In this part a number of issues are discussed that arise when governments debate the use of energy taxes for purposes other than raising revenues. It does not purport to give answers, but explores choices and their implications in a number of policy areas: internalisation, and the limits of taxation as a policy instrument; tax neutrality; taxing energy as a proxy for pollution; and harmonisation and competition policy. Complete exploration of these issues would require quantitative analysis not done for this study; what follows is a qualitative discussion of key issues based on information drawn from the case studies. Nevertheless, these considerations are useful in weighing the relative costs and merits of an energy tax regardless of whether the tax is being levied primarily to raise revenues, to achieve efficient pricing, or as a policy tool.

Internalisation

Current energy prices do not generally reflect the most efficient cost of producing or using energy. There are external costs, such as combustion-related air pollution, land and water pollution and attendant clean-up costs associated with refineries and generating plants, which have not yet been fully internalised by existing environmental measures, energy taxes or energy prices. Such costs are borne elsewhere in the economy and are a source of inefficiency.

Energy taxation can improve economic efficiency by effecting the internalisation, i.e., the absorption, of some of these costs into the price of energy. The advantages to society of internalising these costs include reduced distortions and increased efficiency in pricing and investment, equity for affected third parties, and, not least, the cost minimisation that arises from forcing the producer to be accountable for the required pollution control. But for such taxation to be efficient, costs to be internalised must be carefully defined.

One cannot, for example, appropriately assign the full cost and burden of all air pollution externalities to energy combustion. It is neither efficient nor effective to tax energy to internalise pollution costs not engendered by energy. In this regard, the purpose of the tax-induced internalisation must be clear; otherwise, unintended additional distortions may arise.

First, a distinction must be made between past pollution damages and on-going pollution. Only the latter is appropriate to be internalised into current production costs, even though it may be true that levels of past damages may cause the marginal damage curve of present pollution to be steeper.

In Australia, the United States, Japan and Germany, case study countries where coal is mined, damages due to previous coal mining operations, where not attributable to current producers, become public responsibility. In the U.S., the task of reclaiming abandoned coal lands is given to the states, with funding from a Federal trust fund built by levies on current coal production. In Germany, funding is at least partly federal, but Länder are responsible for coal land reclamation. In Japan, the fund for coal reclamation is subsidised through taxes on other energy forms, namely the petroleum tax and customs duties on oil.

For on-going damages, however, legislation requires current mining operators to absorb reclamation costs, as part of their operations. This is accomplished in these countries primarily by regulation rather than taxation. Nevertheless, mined land reclamation work is generally recognised in the tax codes of these countries as deductible from assessable income.

The same distinction applies to air pollution damages. How will the social costs of past damages be dealt with, and how can incentives be effected to change behaviour which results in pollution? Past air pollution damages including structural deterioration, health damage or others, are generally not assignable, and must be dealt with for the public good through other mechanisms. But for present and future air pollution from on-going energy production and use, there is a legitimate possible role for taxation to effect change.

Where efficient energy pricing and use of resources is the goal of taxation (a classic case of inducing producers to make correct input and investment choices), then the cost to be internalised by the energy tax is that value of the otherwise free resource used in the production process.

In an ideal sense, economically efficient pollution-based energy taxes will help internalise the cost of the damages engendered by the polluter when set at a rate equal to the marginal cost associated with the pollution activity. It follows the axiom, "the polluter pays".

The classic Pigouvian tax, which theoretically optimises social welfare, is one that equates the marginal private cost of production (including the tax) with the marginal social cost of that production. The difficulty here is to define and quantify marginal social cost. There is also the possibility of setting the tax such that marginal cost including tax equals the marginal benefit of abatement. Here one must also define the marginal benefit.

It is tempting to assume that efficient pollution abatement can be achieved by the implementation of a Pigouvian tax. However, construction of a perfect tax requires perfect knowledge. Specifically, construction of an efficient Pigouvian tax requires that the externality-cost or externality-benefit function either be known with certainty or be well-behaved (i.e., adhere to a set of mathematical properties that prevent dual-valued or perverse solutions). Some social cost and social benefit functions fail this test. Thus a typical tax approach (such as a uniform per-unit tax) is unlikely to achieve a Pareto optimal solution, i.e., where it is impossible to make any individual better off without making someone worse off. As a worst case, society could actually be worse off with a Pigouvian tax that imperfectly reflects the marginal social cost.

There is room in between the ideal and the worst case, however, for taxation schemes that achieve some modicum of efficient internalisation without perfect knowledge of marginal social costs and benefits, or marginal social cost and benefit functions, and without serious unintended and damaging side-effects. Clearly, some of the external costs of energy-related pollution are known, for example, and steps taken to internalise these known costs can be assumed to be steps in the right direction. Moreover, if a tax is intended to induce a given level of pollution abatement, then the tax rate need only be set at the marginal abatement cost for the level of pollution which can be tolerated. From the point of view of pure incentive efficiency, it makes little sense to set a tax of $1000 on pollution that costs $0.05 to control to acceptable levels. Governments need to be clear about the purpose and scope of a tax to be able to choose an appropriate option for effective internalisation.

A last question to be addressed is whether energy taxation is necessarily the most effective means of internalising energy-related pollution costs, or perhaps more importantly, achieving a reduction in energy-related pollution. In most OECD countries, the use of taxes instead of regulation to reduce energy related pollution is in incipient stages. At least in the case of some mining damages, and for energy producing facilities in all case study countries to date, regulation has been the tool of choice. In the area of air pollution, enthusiasm for so called "command and control" schemes has given way to a fervour for market-based mechanisms, including taxes. Both regulatory measures and market mechanisms - and mixed systems - have a legitimate place in the repertoire of government policy tools. Mixed systems might involve setting standards by regulation with the efficient meeting of those standards being encouraged by the use of environmental taxes, where an appropriate tax base is available.

As a general rule in choosing among instruments, taxation to reduce pollution is an appropriate tool where a variety of technologies are available to achieve abatement, where pollution effects are dispersed, diverse and difficult to monitor, where sources are numerous, and where the marginal cost of required pollution abatement varies among firms. Under these conditions, taxation tends to achieve lower cost and more efficient compliance than where regulations dictate technology. Taxation is therefore often viewed as a preferred means of dealing with transboundary air pollution and some water pollution problems.

Taxation may not be so appropriate where acceptable control technologies are limited, where pollution effects are localised, where relatively few polluters are involved, or where a given level of compliance is imperative for safety reasons. Regulation in such cases may be more effective and administratively more practical than taxation. Requiring cooling and settling ponds at electric generating plants, waste control at refineries and control of particulates emissions are three examples. In these cases pollution control is internalised by decree, as it were, into the production process. Such regulations, however, while more practical, would still not be as economically efficient as taxes, unless they ensure equalisation of marginal abatement costs among polluters. Penalties for non-compliance and the costs of the control mechanism would be another factor in the over-all efficiency of the regulation.

Note that in the case of energy-related pollution taxes, governments must decide whether to tax energy as a process input or to tax pollution as an activity. The choice should logically be guided by whether the linkage between the taxable event and the pollution is stable across different technologies. (For a more complete discussion of this question, see the section on Energy as a Proxy for Pollution.)

In this regard one should also be mindful that a comprehensive energy tax constitutes a global approach to internalisation, and can have very little to do with the actual external costs associated with various uses of energy. Governments may find it more efficient and more effective in terms of administration, to target taxes or regulations to specific energy users or polluting activities. Both Australia and the United States have used targeted solutions for primarily local or localised national pollution problems. The United States, for example, targets SO_2 pollution with a mixture of regulation, tradeable permits and fees, and levies excise taxes on petroleum to fund oil pollution clean up.

Clearly, there can be serious inefficiencies in mandating pollution control technologies, thereby eliminating economic choices among polluters as to different ways of meeting standards. But an appropriate taxation alternative must be designed to: establish efficient rates or fees consistent with the costs of internalising the social costs associated with the polluting behaviour; avoid exemptions that would weaken or distort desirable behaviour; and target only the behaviour that gives rise to pollution. Otherwise, taxes are incapable of guaranteeing more efficient outcomes than simple regulatory mandates. A well designed tax, however, will generally tend to be more economically efficient than a well designed regulation, for at least two important reasons: first, because taxes provide incentives to compliance, leaving the choice of compliance to the economic actor, and tend to result in least-cost solutions; and second, because construction of regulations requires more perfect knowledge of the affected industries, processes and pollutants than does construction of a tax.

Governments have also traditionally used subsidies, often in the form of tax preferences, to encourage a desired behaviour. Putting aside arguments as to the costs and social inefficiencies of subsidies, the question of interest here is whether subsidies to polluters can effectively achieve the efficient internalisation of pollution costs. The answer must be no. Government compensation to polluters for costs incurred for pollution control does not constitute internalisation, since the cost of the subsidies and hence the pollution control are borne by others, negating any pressure for better resource allocation or efficient pricing.

Subsidised pollution control is also likely to be more costly than pollution control for which the polluter has borne initial financial responsibility and some risk of non-recoupment. Someone spending his own money will always tend to seek least cost method of achieving a given outcome.   Even though a Pigouvian subsidy theoretically exists which would lead to efficient allocation of social costs, subsidies cannot engender a tendency to cost minimisation. To the extent that taxes can be properly constructed and targeted, they tend to do so, and would be preferable as incentives under conditions described above.

Subsidies to energy production as described in the case studies can be instructive for those considering incentive subsidies for pollution control. Subsidising politically desirable behaviour and taxing politically undesirable behaviour without regard for efficiencies, can involve complementary or conflicting efforts. In general, subsidies imply inefficiency and therefore offer a socially costly option for promoting a given behaviour. Subsidies also tend to create privileged interests whose desire for continued subsidies often outlasts the social desirability of subsidization.

Neutrality

The externalities and inefficiencies that exist in energy pricing can be corrected or reduced by taxes. Such remedial taxes should be effective, equitable, and without unintended side-effects, which requires brief consideration of tax neutrality. When considered in the context of a revenue raising tax, and assuming efficient resource pricing, a neutral tax is one which does not change existing patterns of production and consumption, or does not distort otherwise efficient investment decisions. Where externalities and inefficient pricing occur, however, a tax can be used deliberately to alter investment, production and consumption in such a manner as to reduce the inefficiencies and external costs. In this case the tax is not neutral, but nonetheless desirable from society's point of view.

No tax is perfectly neutral. A lump sum tax has only an income effect and no substitution effect. Yet by changing income, even a lump sum tax does have indirect effects on consumption and production.

Taxation can be used to create or reduce distortions in the economic system, sometimes deliberately and sometimes not. Unintended distortions arise largely from imperfect knowledge; deliberate distortions arise from a need to satisfy politically important but not necessarily efficient goals. Taxes levied to fund coal subsidies, such as those currently in effect in Germany and Japan, are an example. There, taxes levied on other forms of energy to maintain regional employment and stability in mining regions result in domestic energy prices far above those on the world markets.

Assuming efficient resource pricing, creating industry-specific tax exemptions, subsidies or privileges benefits one group of taxpayers or exempts them from fiscal obligations to the detriment of others. Even without perfectly efficient resource pricing, discriminatory taxation often creates an implicit subsidy which will affect business and investment decisions in favour of the preferred industry. This is not necessarily a costless strategy.

However, as noted above, there is a justification for corrective taxes where the market equilibrium does not reflect the social optimum. In such cases taxation can be used to correct inefficiencies in the form of externalities, and as an incentive for changing inefficient behaviour. Nevertheless, unless properly structured, taxes intended to be corrective can cause distortions and inefficiencies in their own right. Not all new taxes - even those levied for noble purposes - will, by definition, be corrective. Taxes creating distortions in this context would include those aimed at changing efficient but politically undesirable behaviour.

Revenue neutrality in tax reform should not be confused with the notion of a neutral tax. Revenue neutrality implies changing tax levels, tax rates or the tax base without changing total revenues, or in some instances, without changing the amount of revenues collected from a certain group of taxpayers. Some governments are considering broad tax reform to accommodate increased energy or environmental taxes in a revenue neutral context.

The recent reform of energy excise taxes in Denmark is an illustration of tax reform that includes revenue neutrality. The over-all level of the new excise taxes is largely unchanged from the previous excise taxes. Households pay slightly more in taxes on electricity and on coal, but tax levels for oil and gas are unchanged. As with the previous excise scheme, rebates on the new excise taxes will be available to industry for both the energy and the CO_2-related components of the new taxes. Since relative fuel prices remain largely unchanged, additional price-induced fuel-switching may be small, at least in the short run.

There is inherently no conflict between the notion of revenue neutrality and the Polluter Pays Principle (PPP) subscribed to by OECD countries. The PPP requires that the burden of external costs be shifted to those who cause them. Total revenue can be kept unchanged while shifting this burden through tax reform.

In theory, a tax which induces proper cost internalisation results in efficiency gains which do not require compensation. Compensation or redistribution of income would not be required because society would benefit from an over-all improvement in efficiency. However, if policy makers are more interested in the redistributive effects of a tax than in its efficiency, they could take measures to mitigate the distributional effect of a tax, though this could also lessen its corrective effects.

There is a risk that earmarking or compensatory adjustments made to achieve revenue neutrality could weaken the incentive effect of a tax on polluters. Such measures would also reinforce inefficient pricing of investments and other activities, creating distortions in other sectors or in the implementation of other policies. There are proposals, for example, to collect pollution taxes and earmark the revenues to subsidise pollution control investments. Such earmarking would reduce the incentive effect of a corrective tax on the behaviour of the firm. Compensatory tax adjustments that leave a firm's total tax burden unchanged but alter its tax base, would have more of an incentive effect than compensation through earmarking, but still less than a tax which reflected all costs more accurately.

Appropriate Proxies

Governments are concerned, for a variety of reasons, about the impact of pollution-related taxes on the economic well-being of affected polluters. Some of this concern might be allayed in the case of pollution-related energy taxes, if governments were to clearly divide energy taxes from pollution-related taxes instead of imposing the latter as part of existing energy tax structures. One possible approach would be to restructure energy taxes purely as revenue-raising excise taxes and to impose pollution-related taxes on top of these local excises. The pollution-related taxes would reflect local externalities, and include, if one chose, taxes aimed at more global energy-related pollution, such as a harmonised, strictly carbon-related tax. The recent Danish reform of energy taxes is a pioneer step in this direction. Such a restructuring, however, highlights the importance of knowing when and to what extent energy taxes can appropriately and efficiently be used as a proxy for direct taxes on pollution.

Taxes on energy consumption or fuel inputs are sometimes effectively used as proxies for taxes on emissions or pollutants, but the effectiveness of such proxies varies from country to country, and is largely dependent on elasticities of demand and technology. Where no technology exists for emissions monitoring or abatement, input taxes may be particularly useful proxies for emissions. Such a tax does not directly encourage greater pollution abatement. Rather, to the extent that taxes raise energy prices they will affect some reduction in taxed energy use and so some reduction in energy-related pollution. Tax-induced reductions in energy consumption may also translate into greater efficiency in energy use; or a different fuel mix, if substitution is possible and where taxes change relative fuel prices (reducing, e.g., the cost of lower sulfur or less carbon-intensive fuels); or into a lower level of productive activity that uses energy as an input. All three outcomes would presumably lead to less energy-related pollution.

Taxing proxies generally assumes at least three things. First, there must be some direct link between the activity taxed and the activity to be discouraged. In the case of energy, the assumption is that there is a direct link between fuel purchases and combustion-related pollution emissions. Second, taxing pollution directly must be impractical because monitoring is considered difficult or cost-ineffective. There is concern, for example, that energy users are too numerous and/or mobile to monitor their pollution. Third, there must be little effective scope for direct abatement of the undesirable behaviour.

Consider each assumption in the light of the energy input/pollution output relationship. First, on the question of linkage, environmental tax experts agree that inefficiencies arise when linkage between the taxed activity and the pollution activity is insufficiently close, or where technological options for pollution control include effluent cleaning technologies. (See, in this regard, the OECD publication, *Taxation and the Environment*). Inefficiencies may also arise even if the linkage is exact. This is particularly true for fuel-related pollution. Having already paid a tax on the energy input (based on sulfur content, carbon content, heat value or whatever), the consumer has little incentive to invest further in pollution control equipment to reduce emissions. The pollution-related costs that the polluter pays are not affected by improved pollution abatement efforts, yet abatement might be a more efficient, effective and less costly option than paying a fuel tax. Moreover, the pollution costs seen by society are obviously affected by control efforts, and that is the striking inefficiency to which proxy tax schemes are vulnerable. In this case, taxing the input as a proxy for pollution rewards those making no effort towards pollution abatement (other than perhaps initial fuel choice).

There is a similar disincentive to invest in research on abatement, since the financial benefit of its application is not certain. Thus, there is little or no incentive to break the link - precise or tenuous - between energy use and pollution.   By contrast, focusing the incentive system precisely on environmental objectives   eg. curbing airborne emissions, reducing waterborne discharges, etc. - reduces such distortions in economic behaviour and environmental performance.

Where monitoring or abatement technologies exist (or can be reasonably expected to develop), the denomination of energy use as a proxy for pollution may not be the most apt proxy relationship available.   In these cases, it is more efficient and effective to tax the pollution.

In both Germany and Australia, efforts are being made in this direction. In Australia, a general tax on commercially-used motor fuel is being replaced by a more direct tax based on measured pollution damages caused by heavy vehicles. In Germany, where motor vehicle tax rates are already intended to reflect at least roughly the pollution capacity of the vehicle, a more direct tax on measured pollution emissions is being considered to replace the present scheme.

The second assumption suggests that direct government monitoring of pollutants is a necessary condition for implementing a tax to control emissions. Yet there are mechanisms available to eliminate the need for government monitoring. One more novel approach could be called the "presumption principle" of polluting activity; this presumes that ownership of equipment is tantamount to intent to use it, and if the equipment is potentially polluting, its use constitutes an intent to pollute. The potentially polluting item is therefore taxed up front at the time of acquisition, at a level consonant with internalising maximum possible pollution costs. The tax is refunded on evidence of actual pollution levels less than the maximum posited. This principle can be applied in designing pre-paid self-monitoring pollution taxes for energy-related pollution emissions, including greenhouse gases.

The right, but not the obligation, to monitor actual emissions would lie with the consumer who has been taxed in advance on his potential for emissions. If the initial tax is sufficiently high, the refund provides a strong economic incentive for self-monitoring. For most energy-related pollution, such monitoring would not entail radically new monitoring technologies.

Calculating the potential for CO_2 and NO_x emissions from automobile engines, for example, need not entail major technological developments or undue investment. Monitoring could be incorporated into the inspections already required in the United States and Canada, to measure the combustion properties of automobile engines, to enforce a variety of fuel efficiency and pollution abatement programs. As noted earlier, Germany is proposing such a procedure for taxing automobile emissions directly, instead of taxing engine design and vehicle weight as proxies for pollution capabilities.

A self-monitoring pre-paid pollution tax system based on such measurements only requires that automobile owners provide evidence of actual usage of the vehicle at the time of emissions measurement, to secure a partial rebate. Such evidence of usage is readily available from odometer readings taken during annual safety inspections, or from chronometers that log hours of operation for aviation, commercial marine engines or truck fleet operators.

For stationary sources, gas spectroscopy on smokestacks - already developed and in use since the 1970s - permits comparable self-monitoring. Such methods may produce only approximations of actual emissions, but they are more than adequate given the scientific basis on which the greenhouse gas or other emission standards are likely to be set.

A high initial tax might also provide incentives for investment in improved monitoring equipment. Such an incentive system could even bring about more technologically sophisticated monitoring systems where polluters stand to gain net benefits from improved measurement capability.

This presumption/self-monitoring approach is conceptually no different in principle than the application of deposit-refund systems. A deposit-refund system assumes that ownership of certain goods entails the potential for pollution if the goods are not returned or recycled. The incentive not to pollute is in the form of the deposit, paid up front, on the presumption that the item purchased will create pollution. The consumer is responsible for proving he did not pollute, and for triggering the ensuing refund by returning or recycling the item. The burden in effect is shifted to the potential polluter to monitor his own pollution. This motivating self-interest is an important point in the context of enforcement and monitoring procedures, and associated administrative costs. Denmark already makes use of such self-monitoring in its scheme for providing rebates of energy-related excise duties to eligible consumers through the VAT reporting system.

This is not to suggest that such monitoring costs are trivial. They may or may not be. But the question is relative, since costs must be compared to the benefits that can be derived. Nor is the system foolproof: clearly there is always the possibility of cheating, though probably no more so than with other monitoring programs. Nevertheless, potential for distortions in input choices, in missed opportunities in technology development and ensuing economic inefficiency from both these distortions would be less under such a system than under a system of indirect proxy taxes.

The third assumption expands on the suggestion that technology is incapable of adequately monitoring pollution to posit that technology is also incapable - now and for the foreseeable future - of satisfactorily and efficiently providing energy-related pollution abatement, particularly with regard to greenhouse gas emissions. It is somewhat ironic that advocates of alternative (and non-fossil) energy economies as the solution to global warming are willing to assume that technological solutions in those areas will be forthcoming, but are less willing to assume similar, less radical technological developments in the area of environmental controls, monitoring, or emissions abatement.

Technical advances in obtaining electricity from renewable energy sources, transportation from radically more fuel-efficient vehicles or cost-effective mass transit systems may indeed be developed. However, control technologies already exist in most OECD countries for emissions abatement for most energy-related air pollution. And, there are techniques which have already been researched, costed, and reported on under IEA auspices that suggest there will be effective CO_2 and other greenhouse gas abatement technologies available, if only in selected, but significant, applications. (See for example, *Proceedings of First International Conference on Carbon Dioxide Removal*, Pergamon Press, 1992.). Utilities in Japan are already running pilot programs in removal and fixation of CO_2 for power plant emission streams.

This paper does not necessarily advocate adoption of pre-paid, self-monitoring pollution tax systems, but they should not be summarily dismissed. Critical to the success of any incentive tax is the creation of proper incentives. And in this context, the pre-paid self-monitoring tax proposal based on the deposit-refund principle is an interesting way to harness basic economic drives to achieve broader policy objectives. It is also consonant with the above-mentioned option of separating pollution-abatement incentive taxes from energy excises.

Harmonisation

Concern about potential economic side-effects of taxes aimed at reducing pollution has also stimulated great interest in the question of harmonisation. The desirability of harmonising policy goals and/or instruments is discussed most often in the context of discussions about global environmental problems, and the use of environment-related energy taxes as pollution abatement incentives. Whether harmonisation is appropriate or necessary in a given instance will depend largely on how pollution costs are defined, and whether one is intending harmonisation of goals or of instruments.

If the pollution problems to be internalised are international or transboundary in nature, then the most efficient way to achieve a given reduction in global emissions is through a common international tax tending to equalise the marginal cost of emission abatement across the world. Equalising marginal abatement costs, however, does not imply equal impacts on all countries or industries.

By contrast, if the pollution externalities to be internalised by a tax are national or local in nature, then the tax should reflect national or local policy needs. Such taxes will promote efficient abatement by tending to equalise the marginal cost of abatement among all polluters subject to the tax. The cost of compliance with pollution standards and taxes in other countries are not directly relevant to the imposition of the tax. Nor is harmonisation of pollution standards or taxes between countries required to achieve efficiency.

It is also important to define the target vehicle for harmonisation. For policy makers this usually implies a choice between harmonising tax instruments or trying to harmonise results. From a purely economic perspective, the logical vehicle for harmonisation would be a tax to achieve a single outcome, namely convergence of the marginal cost of the behaviour being taxed. Different and important consequences result, depending on which target vehicle is selected.

In the case of concern over CO_2 emissions, for example, harmonisation of emissions reductions at or to specified uniform levels will almost certainly require different measures, including differently structured taxes and different tax rates, even among the case study countries. By contrast, harmonisation of instruments, i.e., the mechanisms to achieve emissions reductions, could produce identical carbon-related taxes and tax rates but would almost surely lead to different levels of emission reductions in different countries. Harmonisation of global marginal abatement costs through a common global tax would lead to the most efficient reduction of CO_2 emissions, but would produce very different emission reduction levels and impose very different costs on different countries. Such results are not likely to be politically attractive, which may militate towards the choice of some other target for harmonisation. Nevertheless, this last approach provides the most compelling context for efficient coordinated action against global pollution.

Harmonisation of goals is a commonly accepted political purpose and outcome of international agreements, including those dealing with global pollution. However, stringent requirements for uniform outcomes expressed in terms of emissions reductions or emissions levels, and which do not take into account national circumstances, can result in less efficient, more costly compliance for international goals because the marginal cost of compliance with the emissions regulations or pollution standards will vary from country to country. To the extent that the implementation of rigidly harmonised international environmental protection schemes result in distorted investments at the national level, they can also be detrimental to both the cost and the success of national environmental protection or development programs.

One compromise approach which seeks to mitigate these effects is to harmonise environmental quality objectives, and then let each country find the most efficient means of achieving them. This would eliminate some of the inefficiencies that would arise within a country, but would not permit the capture of the potential for international efficiencies arising from the existence of different marginal costs in different countries.

As for the abatement of environmental damages that do not cross national boundaries, it is logical, efficient and socially beneficial for governments to tax an activity whenever the external costs engendered by that activity exceed its positive contribution to the social welfare function. In the case of energy, this means that it may make sense in some circumstances for governments to tax, *inter alia,* the industrial use of energy, even where this might mean some loss of energy intensive industries in the industrial mix. Each government clearly must set energy- and environment-related taxes and other measures according to national priorities, and reflecting domestic energy and environment profiles, including marginal abatement cost and damage functions, and taking into account the elasticities of energy demand and supply.

Consider, for example, the attempts to date by OECD countries to reduce energy-related (not CO_2) pollution through increasing the efficiency of energy use. Energy consumption varies among countries to reflect climate, population distribution, and industry mix without bearing any necessary relationship to the economic or technical efficiency of energy use. Scandinavia may have very efficient buildings and heating systems and still consume more energy for space heating than OECD countries on the Mediterranean Sea. In France, air pollution from power generation is far less of a problem than water pollution or motor vehicle pollution arising from relatively dirty fuel and limited installation of auto pollution control equipment. In the US, with relatively clean fuel and stringent auto pollution control requirements, motor vehicle-related pollution is more a function of vehicle fuel efficiency and miles driven. A single uniform tax, incentive, or pollution control scheme would operate with very different results if applied to such different energy economies.

Competition and Harmonisation

The growing globalisation of commerce and competition, along with the rise of free trade zones and the elimination of trade restrictions, have given great impetus to pressures for harmonisation of policy goals and measures being discussed to manage international aspects of environmental problems.

Current political interest in harmonisation has been given particular urgency by efforts of the European Community to forge a single internal market, while reflecting differing national economic or environmental concerns and profiles. In the past, countries could protect their own chosen level of environmental quality, enforce their own environmental measures, limit the effects of (or at least capture the rents from) industry relocation, and exert pressure on other governments to impose similar measures, through the use of trade restrictions, especially import taxes or tariffs. Such tariffs, where designed to be equivalent to taxes levied on domestic products, can be viewed at least arguably as being consistent with the GATT. These devices, however, are not available to countries sharing a free trade zone. Harmonisation then becomes an attractive if not necessary alternative to preserve a country's competitive position and terms of trade, without necessarily sacrificing environmental or other policy standards.

The relative tax burdens of competing firms can be a factor in their competitive positions, as well as in investment and industrial location decisions. Where a country contemplates regulatory measures or taxes for environmental benefit, it therefore must (or believes it must) consider the effect of these measures on the relative costs and competitive position of its effected industries, *vis à vis*, those of competitors whose national governments impose different measures, or do not intervene at all.

However, the implied underlying assumption, that the effects of government intervention will be detrimental to the effected industries, does not necessarily hold true. Presumably such interventions will increase social and economic efficiency, and may force technological innovations that improve the internationally competitive position of national companies.

Concern by effected industries over their absolute tax burden, industry threats of relocation based on relative tax burdens, and arguments about ability to compete give rise to two kinds of demands.

First, concerned governments may seek policy or tax harmonisation with their trading partners to reduce the possibility of industrial relocation and/or loss of export market share. Such concerns have also given rise to pressures by nations with high-priced energy for others to adjust upwards their energy pricing regimes or their energy price levels. In the case of energy taxes within the European Community, for example, it is interesting to note that countries advocating harmonisation most vociferously (and uniform carbon-related taxes where these are under consideration), are generally those countries with the highest energy taxes, who do not wish to lower those taxes but are afraid of losing market share.

Governments should remember, in this regard, that harmonisation of tax instruments will in fact impose different costs on different competitors. Since the marginal damage from pollution differs among countries with different energy use and pollution profiles, national responses to harmonised tax rates will differ, as will the amount and cost of pollution control achieved. Governments should also note that, in the case of incentive taxes, the ultimate burden of the tax is to some extent within the control of the taxpayer, who can reduce that burden by changing behaviour. The impact on location and investment decisions is therefore different from that of a more purely revenue raising tax.

The second type of demand comes from industries concerned about their competitive standing. They will seek - and obtain - exemptions from national taxes or other such national measures. In the case of energy-related taxes, many schemes shield energy-intensive industries from a significant share of energy taxes, sometimes reflecting mercantilist concerns about the competitive position of national industries in international markets. The Danish carbon-based energy excise scheme is a case in point among the case study countries.

Governments do need to be concerned about efficient targeting and equitable distribution of the tax burden, particularly in trying to design effective incentive taxes. However, such exemptions tend to undermine both the effectiveness and the perceived equity of the tax, and frustrate the process of changing undesirable behaviour or internalising external costs. This is particularly the case if the tax is intended to improve national welfare and efficiency.

Such exemptions can also introduce new distortions in investment. In such instances, there is little effective difference between exempting industries from environment-related taxes and exempting them from pollution control requirements. In either case relative costs and prices will be skewed, and, whatever pollution-reducing incentive effect was intended to result from the tax or other measure, will be lost on the exempted decision maker. Trade in both internal and external markets will be distorted.

One of the dangers in accommodating such concerns is that harmonisation can be used as a protectionist instrument. In the interest of managing markets, differences instead of inefficiencies can be the targets of harmonisation, with a goal to minimising relative competitive advantages. This might be done to protect the market shares of competing national industries, but taken to its ultimate logical conclusion, it would also reduce the advantages of trade.

This is not to imply, however, that all changes in trade resulting from government interventions or environmental measures will cause trade distortions. That would presume that existing trade patterns are optimally efficient and environmentally desirable, which they are not. Changes in trade resulting from tax reforms or other environmental measures may in fact constitute efficiency gains. Harmonisation impeding such efficiency gains is not desirable.

CO_2 taxes - a special case

The strongest drive for a globally harmonised energy-related tax has come from those urging a prompt and harmonised reduction in CO_2 emissions. The difficulties in harmonising environmentally oriented taxes in this respect are clearly illustrated by the efforts of governments to devise and implement a global scheme of carbon-based taxes, as a proxy for taxes on carbon dioxide emissions. (Note, however, that the difficulties associated with harmonisation are separate from those associated with defining appropriate proxies discussed above.) The generally agreed approach is to tax the carbon content of fossil-fuels and hence reduce the use of carbon-based fuels in order, ultimately, to reduce carbon dioxide emissions from energy combustion.

The estimated level of tax required to effect a significant reduction in CO_2 emissions is high, and varies from country to country depending on energy mix, existing energy taxes, elasticities of demand, and industrial and sectoral infrastructure. Because required tax levels for significant CO_2 reductions are so high[1], governments are concerned about the macro-economic impacts of a carbon tax: inflation, distortions in investment, dead weight losses to GDP, reduced growth and unemployment. Industries are seriously concerned about the competitive implications of a carbon tax for their relative market shares, domestically as well as internationally. These concerns would be exacerbated if vastly different energy tax rates are required to achieve uniform emissions reductions.

As noted above, the ultimately efficient carbon-based tax would be one that harmonised marginal costs of achieving a given level of CO_2 emissions abatement throughout the world. This, too, would impose different costs on different countries and would achieve different emissions levels in different countries, but would minimise global abatement costs. Emissions would be reduced first and most in those countries where reduction is the cheapest. (Note that efficient cost solutions can also be approached by using a global tradeable emissions permits system, though administratively this would probably be more difficult to apply.)

The first question regarding carbon-related taxes is whether to harmonise at all. Are governments willing to impose economic and social changes required by harmonisation? Should they? Do they know the costs and benefits of imposing harmonised carbon taxes (one problem being, for example, that costs will be obvious in the short run, but benefits will not appear until perhaps much later). Can harmonisation be done in a way that is both efficient and within the bounds of political acceptability?

The next question is whether to harmonise the instrument (i.e., the tax), or the results (i.e., the level of pollution reduction). Each choice dictates vastly different results. If a uniform harmonised carbon tax were imposed in the five case study countries, it is reasonable to expect different changes in energy prices, different changes in energy consumption patterns and different changes in CO_2 emissions levels, given the different tax

---

1 See, for example, the work described in "An Analysis of Energy Policy Measures and Their Impact on CO_2 Emissions", IEA, Paris, June 1991, as cited in Part II.

regimes, elasticities, fuel mix and infrastructures in these countries, and the different relative burdens of energy taxes on final prices.

If results are harmonised in the form of CO_2 emission reductions, then governments will still have to accept different levels of taxation and different relative fuel prices. This implies different costs for competing national industries. As seen in Part I, however, relative fuel prices and energy tax burdens are already different in the case study countries. There is nothing inequitable or undesirable about such differences, and carbon taxes should not be used to harmonise them away.

Some governments might seek to equalise or compensate for tax-induced relative price changes, through exemptions or adjustment to other taxes. It is unclear without quantitative analysis, what other kinds of adjustments governments might make in direct taxes or other costs imposed on industry if a given level of carbon tax is imposed, or how important the competitive implications of such a tax would be, given the range of adjustments possible in other areas. It is also unclear how environmentally effective such a tax would be, given various compensatory adjustments. But it is clear that countries which exempt industry from carbon-related energy taxes will see less reduction in fuel use and in emissions than would otherwise be obtained with more universal application of the tax.

Is it even possible to design a CO_2 tax that is both effective and politically acceptable? Whether instruments or results or marginal costs are ultimately the target of harmonisation, different countries and industries will experience a wide variety of costs and relative prices, not all of which will be politically acceptable. If governments are obliged to respond to political and mercantilist concerns by exempting certain industries from the tax or by otherwise compensating them for its impact, they will inevitably reduce the effectiveness of the tax. Exemptions or compensation, in some cases, could be considered a reward to polluters, thereby standing the "polluter pays principle" on its head.

Conclusions

Governments tax along a policy continuum, ranging from measures aimed primarily at raising general revenues (but which also affect prices and behaviour) to measures aimed primarily at promoting or discouraging specific behaviour (but which also raise revenues).

Energy taxes have been used for a number of purposes, and their potential use as a policy tool seems to be expanding. Of great interest is the use of energy taxes to reduce energy consumption, either for purposes of enhanced security of energy supply, or to reduce the undesirable environmental side-effects of energy use.

Governments may choose, for administrative and political or policy reasons, to tax energy rather than pollution as a means of pollution control. Despite their potential for inefficiencies, energy taxes do raise energy prices, and so effect some reduction in energy use and some reduction in energy-related pollution. This may imply some productive and investment inefficiencies in the economy along with some efficiency gains due to internalisation of certain pollution costs.

Energy-related pollution can also and perhaps more efficiently be reduced by taxing pollution instead of energy use, which tends to be a desirable activity aside from the environmental externalities it produces. Direct pollution taxes are less familiar, and may require more careful structuring at least initially, though the ultimate gain in efficiency of pollution abatement may be worth the effort.

In either case, efficient and equitable structuring of energy-based incentive taxes will require attention to concerns including proper internalisation, harmonisation and targeting of taxes.

MAIN SALES OUTLETS OF OECD PUBLICATIONS
PRINCIPAUX POINTS DE VENTE DES PUBLICATIONS DE L'OCDE

ARGENTINA – ARGENTINE
Carlos Hirsch S.R.L.
Galería Güemes, Florida 165, 4° Piso
1333 Buenos Aires   Tel. (1) 331.1787 y 331.2391
Telefax: (1) 331.1787

AUSTRALIA – AUSTRALIE
D.A. Information Services
648 Whitehorse Road, P.O.B 163
Mitcham, Victoria 3132   Tel. (03) 873.4411
Telefax: (03) 873.5679

AUSTRIA – AUTRICHE
Gerold & Co.
Graben 31
Wien I   Tel. (0222) 533.50.14

BELGIUM – BELGIQUE
Jean De Lannoy
Avenue du Roi 202
B-1060 Bruxelles   Tel. (02) 538.51.69/538.08.41
Telefax: (02) 538.08.41

CANADA
Renouf Publishing Company Ltd.
1294 Algoma Road
Ottawa, ON K1B 3W8   Tel. (613) 741.4333
Telefax: (613) 741.5439
Stores:
61 Sparks Street
Ottawa, ON K1P 5R1   Tel. (613) 238.8985
211 Yonge Street
Toronto, ON M5B 1M4   Tel. (416) 363.3171

Les Éditions La Liberté Inc.
3020 Chemin Sainte-Foy
Sainte-Foy, PQ G1X 3V6   Tel. (418) 658.3763
Telefax: (418) 658.3763

Federal Publications
165 University Avenue
Toronto, ON M5H 3B8   Tel. (416) 581.1552
Telefax: (416) 581.1743

Les Publications Fédérales
1185 Avenue de l'Université
Montréal, PQ H3B 3A7   Tel. (514) 954.1633
Telefax : (514) 954.1633

CHINA – CHINE
China National Publications Import
Export Corporation (CNPIEC)
16 Gongti E. Road, Chaoyang District
P.O. Box 88 or 50
Beijing 100704 PR   Tel. (01) 506.6688
Telefax: (01) 506.3101

DENMARK – DANEMARK
Munksgaard Export and Subscription Service
35, Nørre Søgade, P.O. Box 2148
DK-1016 København K   Tel. (33) 12.85.70
Telefax: (33) 12.93.87

FINLAND – FINLANDE
Akateeminen Kirjakauppa
Keskuskatu 1, P.O. Box 128
00100 Helsinki   Tel. (358 0) 12141
Telefax: (358 0) 121.4441

FRANCE
OECD/OCDE
Mail Orders/Commandes par correspondance:
2, rue André-Pascal
75775 Paris Cedex 16   Tel. (33-1) 45.24.82.00
Telefax: (33-1) 45.24.81.76   or (33-1) 45.24.85.00
Telex: 640048 OCDE

OECD Bookshop/Librairie de l'OCDE :
33, rue Octave-Feuillet
75016 Paris   Tel. (33-1) 45.24.81.67
(33-1) 45.24.81.81

Documentation Française
29, quai Voltaire
75007 Paris   Tel. 40.15.70.00
Gibert Jeune (Droit-Économie)
6, place Saint-Michel
75006 Paris   Tel. 43.25.91.19
Librairie du Commerce International
10, avenue d'Iéna
75016 Paris   Tel. 40.73.34.60
Librairie Dunod
Université Paris-Dauphine
Place du Maréchal de Lattre de Tassigny
75016 Paris   Tel. 47.27.18.56
Librairie Lavoisier
11, rue Lavoisier
75008 Paris   Tel. 42.65.39.95
Librairie L.G.D.J. - Montchrestien
20, rue Soufflot
75005 Paris   Tel. 46.33.89.85
Librairie des Sciences Politiques
30, rue Saint-Guillaume
75007 Paris   Tel. 45.48.36.02
P.U.F.
49, boulevard Saint-Michel
75005 Paris   Tel. 43.25.83.40
Librairie de l'Université
12a, rue Nazareth
13100 Aix-en-Provence   Tel. (16) 42.26.18.08
Documentation Française
165, rue Garibaldi
69003 Lyon   Tel. (16) 78.63.32.23
Librairie Decitre
29, place Bellecour
69002 Lyon   Tel. (16) 72.40.54.54

GERMANY – ALLEMAGNE
OECD Publications and Information Centre
August-Bebel-Allee 6
D-W 5300 Bonn 2   Tel. (0228) 959.120
Telefax: (0228) 959.12.17

GREECE – GRÈCE
Librairie Kauffmann
Mavrokordatou 9
106 78 Athens   Tel. 322.21.60
Telefax: 363.39.67

HONG-KONG
Swindon Book Co. Ltd.
13–15 Lock Road
Kowloon, Hong Kong   Tel. 366.80.31
Telefax: 739.49.75

HUNGARY – HONGRIE
Euro Info Service
kázmér u.45
1121 Budapest   Tel. (1) 182.00.44
Telefax : (1) 182.00.44

ICELAND – ISLANDE
Mál Mog Menning
Laugavegi 18, Pósthólf 392
121 Reykjavik   Tel. 162.35.23

INDIA – INDE
Oxford Book and Stationery Co.
Scindia House
New Delhi 110001   Tel.(11) 331.5896/5308
Telefax: (11) 332.5993
17 Park Street
Calcutta 700016   Tel. 240832

INDONESIA – INDONÉSIE
Pdii-Lipi
P.O. Box 269/JKSMG/88
Jakarta 12790   Tel. 583467
Telex: 62 875

IRELAND – IRLANDE
TDC Publishers – Library Suppliers
12 North Frederick Street
Dublin 1   Tel. 74.48.35/74.96.77
Telefax: 74.84.16

ISRAEL
Electronic Publications only
Publications électroniques seulement
Sophist Systems Ltd.
71 Allenby Street
Tel-Aviv 65134   Tel. 3-29.00.21
Telefax: 3-29.92.39

ITALY – ITALIE
Libreria Commissionaria Sansoni
Via Duca di Calabria 1/1
50125 Firenze   Tel. (055) 64.54.15
Telefax: (055) 64.12.57
Via Bartolini 29
20155 Milano   Tel. (02) 36.50.83
Editrice e Libreria Herder
Piazza Montecitorio 120
00186 Roma   Tel. 679.46.28
Telefax: 678.47.51
Libreria Hoepli
Via Hoepli 5
20121 Milano   Tel. (02) 86.54.46
Telefax: (02) 805.28.86
Libreria Scientifica
Dott. Lucio de Biasio 'Aeiou'
Via Coronelli, 6
20146 Milano   Tel. (02) 48.95.45.52
Telefax: (02) 48.95.45.48

JAPAN – JAPON
OECD Publications and Information Centre
Landic Akasaka Building
2-3-4 Akasaka, Minato-ku
Tokyo 107   Tel. (81.3) 3586.2016
Telefax: (81.3) 3584.7929

KOREA – CORÉE
Kyobo Book Centre Co. Ltd.
P.O. Box 1658, Kwang Hwa Moon
Seoul   Tel. 730.78.91
Telefax: 735.00.30

MALAYSIA – MALAISIE
Co-operative Bookshop Ltd.
University of Malaya
P.O. Box 1127, Jalan Pantai Baru
59700 Kuala Lumpur
Malaysia   Tel. 756.5000/756.5425
Telefax: 757.3661

MEXICO – MEXIQUE
Revistas y Periodicos Internacionales S.A. de C.V.
Florencia 57 - 1004
Mexico, D.F. 06600   Tel. 207.81.00
Telefax : 208.39.79

NETHERLANDS – PAYS-BAS
SDU Uitgeverij
Christoffel Plantijnstraat 2
Postbus 20014
2500 EA's-Gravenhage   Tel. (070 3) 78.99.11
Voor bestellingen: Tel. (070 3) 78.98.80
Telefax: (070 3) 47.63.51

NEW ZEALAND
NOUVELLE-ZÉLANDE
Legislation Services
P.O. Box 12418
Thorndon, Wellington   Tel. (04) 496.5652
Telefax: (04) 496.5698